D1081250

WHERE
IN THE
WORLD
?

Christine McClymont
James Barry
Berenice Wood

Published in 1995 simultaneously by:

Nelson Canada,   *and*   The Wright Group
A division of Thomson   19201 – 120th Avenue NE
   Canada Limited   Bothell, Washington
1120 Birchmount Road   98011-9512
Scarborough, Ontario   U.S.A.
M1K 5G4
Canada

ISBN 0-17-604721-2   ISBN 0-17-604722-0

1 2 3 4 5 /WC/ 98 97 96 95 94   1 2 3 4 5 /WC/ 98 97 96 95 94

I(T)P ™
International Thomson Publishing
The ITP logo is a trademark under licence

Project Manager/Development: Lana Kong
Supervising Editor, Production: Sandra Manley
Sr. Composition Analyst: Alicja Jamorski
Art Direction: Liz Nyman
Cover Design: Katharine Lapins
Cover Illustration: Tomio Nitto
Production Coordinator: Renate McCloy

Printed and bound in Canada

Canadian Cataloguing in Publication Data

Main entry under title:

Where in the world?

(Nelson mini-anthologies)
ISBN 0-17-604721-2

1. Readers (Secondary). 2. Readers – Geography.
3. Geography – Literary collections.   I. McClymont, Christine.
II. Barry, James, 1939–   . III. Wood, Berenice L. (Berenice
Laura), 1947– .

PE1121.W44   1994   808′.0427   C94-932146-X

Series Review Panel

Lynn Archer, Helping Teacher, Surrey School District No. 36, Surrey, B.C.

Sandie Bender, Academic Coordinator, Carleton Roman Catholic School Board, Nepean, Ont.

Mary Cahill, Resource Teacher, Winnipeg School Division No. 1, Winnipeg, Man.

Ross Elliott, Assistant Superintendent for Curriculum and Instruction, Avalon North Integrated School Board, Spaniards Bay, Nfld.

Bob Ernest, English Consultant, Waterloo Board of Education, Waterloo, Ont.

Kathleen Gregory, Teacher, Sooke School District No. 62, Victoria, B.C.

Dennis Haworth, Teacher, St. Albert Protestant Separate School District No. 6, St. Albert, Alta.

Maureen Kennedy, Teacher, School District No. 17, Oromocto, N.B.

Carole Kent, English Consultant, along with Teachers of the Halton Roman Catholic School Board, Burlington, Ont.

Regina Maher, Teacher, Saskatoon Roman Catholic Separate School Division No. 20, Saskatoon, Sask.

David Skeaff, Teacher, Northumberland and Newcastle Board of Education, Cobourg, Ont.

Mary Sullivan, Program Facilitator, Curriculum, County of Parkland No. 31, Stony Plain, Alta.

Carol Symons, Language Arts Consultant, Edmonton Public School Board, Edmonton, Alta.

Clevie Wall, Secondary Consultant, Dartmouth District School Board, Dartmouth, N.S.

Chelvin Hall, Anti-racism Consultant, Toronto, Ont.

Antonio J. Tavares, Multicultural Education Specialist, Languages and Anti-racism Education, Manitoba Department of Education and Training, Winnipeg, Man.

Helene Yellowlees, Co-ordinator and Teacher of Interdisciplinary Studies, North York Board of Education, North York, Ont.

Dr. Dana Callen, Instructional Services for Leon County Schools, Tallahassee, Fla.

Dr. Michael F. Opitz, University of Southern Colorado, Pueblo, Colo.

Dr. Judith N. Thelen, Frostburg State University, Frostburg, Md.

Table of Contents

1

GLOBE-TROTTING

2

FESTIVAL TIME!

3

FROM ART TO ARCHITECTURE

4

WAYS OF THE WILD

5

HOMECOMING

Photographs follow page 72.

Globe-trotting

▲ ▶ ▼ ▶ ▲ ▼ ▶ ▼ ▲ ▼ ▶ ▼ ▲ ▼ ▶ ▼ ▲ ▶

Paper Boats

Day by day I float my paper boats one by
    one down the running stream.
In big black letters I write my name on
    them and the name of the village
    where I live.
I hope that someone in some strange land
    will find them and know who I am.
I load my little boats with shiuli flowers
    from our garden, and hope that these
    blooms of the dawn will be carried
    safely to land in the night.
I launch my paper boats and look into the
    sky and see the little clouds setting
    their white bulging sails.
I know not what playmate of mine in the
    sky sends them down the air to race
    with my boats!

When night comes I bury my face in my
arms and dream that my paper boats
float on and on under the midnight
stars.
The fairies of sleep are sailing in them, and
the lading is their baskets full of
dreams.

Rabindranath Tagore

▲ ▼ ▶ ▼ ▶ ▲ ▼ ▶ ▼ ▶ ▲ ▼ ▶ ▼ ▶ ▲ ▼ ▶ ▼ ▶ ▶

▲ ▼ ▶ ▼ ▶ ▲ ▼ ▶ ▼ ▶ ▲ ▼ ▶ ▼ ▶ ▲ ▼ ▶ ▼ ▶ ▶

TASHKENT

by Tim Wynne-Jones

Faraway places with unfamiliar names—they seemed to be the only thing that helped Fletcher survive his mysterious illness.

One day, for no particular reason Fletcher pasted the names of a lot of exotic places on his chest and stomach. His mother and father were chatting in the kitchen when he went to show them.

"Oh, no," said his mother. "Fletcher's got the dreaded little-bits-of-paper-with-writing-on-it disease."

"There's been quite an outbreak of it," said his father, leaning close to inspect Fletcher's remarkably decorated torso. "Zagreb?"

"They're all places I'd like to go some day," said Fletcher, looking down at his chest. "When I'm older."

His mother joined in the examination. "Ibadan. Where's that?"

"It's the second largest city in Nigeria," said

Fletcher, pressing down on that piece of paper. It was peeling already. He didn't want the names to fall off just yet, though they felt funny on his skin now that the glue had dried.

Dad went to refill his coffee cup. "How long is this malady going to last?"

Mom, always more matter-of-fact, said, "What about gym?"

"Gym's not until Thursday," said Fletcher. "They should have all fallen off by then."

Even as he spoke, Ibadan fluttered to the floor. They all watched. Mom picked it up but wasn't sure what you did when the second biggest city in Nigeria fell on your kitchen floor. She handed it to Fletcher, who crumpled it up and put it in his pants pocket.

"The last place left is the first place I'm going to travel to when I'm old enough," said Fletcher.

Dad stopped pouring his coffee for a moment. "So it's sort of a contest?" he said.

Mom frowned. "Does this contest stretch all the way down into your shorts?"

"Nope," said Fletcher. He turned and carefully headed out of the kitchen, walking like a robot so as not to disturb the possibilities stuck all over him. "That wouldn't be fair."

"Not fair?"

Fletcher turned at the door, twisting slowly from the waist. "I mean, if I put—let's say—Bilbao on my heel, it would come off the first time I pulled on my sock, right?" His mother and father nodded.

"And if I put Uppsala on my bum—"

"We get the idea," said Mom.

"Yes," said Dad. "Now it all makes perfect sense."

Fletcher smiled. He had a winning smile.

When he was nine, Fletcher almost died. He got sick, and it wasn't the little-bits-of-paper-with-writing-on-it disease. Nobody was able to figure out what it was. He just got weaker and weaker.

The medical people did X rays and found nothing. They did "blood-work," as they called it, and found nothing. They did ultrasound; they squilched goop all over his abdomen, and a technician pushed something like a computer mouse through the goop. Somehow or other, Fletcher's insides appeared on a TV monitor. The technician watched the monitor closely. So did Fletcher.

"That ugly thing must be it," he said at one point.

"That's your kidney," the technician said. "It looks fine to me."

Fletcher asked the technician if he could tune in the Cosby Show. The technician laughed. The ultrasound found nothing.

Fletcher had to be very brave because, as far as he knew, he was dying. He seemed to have no immunities to anything. They tested for AIDS, but it wasn't AIDS. They wanted to open him up and see what was going on, but by then Fletcher had become too weak, and the doctors were afraid that the operation would kill him. That's when Fletcher learned the expression "between a rock and a hard place."

As the months of his mysterious illness dragged on and he sank lower and lower, he talked to his mother a lot about death. Death became a place. Like Death Valley in California. Or Death Valley Junction, the last place before Death Valley. It didn't hurt so much to think about death if it was somewhere to visit, even if it was quite far away from anywhere else. That's when Fletcher started looking at atlases and travel books a lot and thinking about exotic places that weren't quite so hard to take.

"Why are you clutching your gut?" said Shlomo when they were walking to school the next day. Shlomo was Fletcher's best friend. He looked worried.

Fletcher explained about the exotic places stuck all over his body. Shlomo looked relieved.

"I thought I saw a little piece of paper drop off you a while back."

"Did you happen to notice what it said?" Fletcher asked. Even though he had slept on his back with only his sheet over him, he had lost both Singapore and Tunapuna during the night.

Shlomo hadn't noticed what city it was. Fletcher hoped it wasn't somewhere warm. The warm places were dropping like flies. Not that he really cared which city won. He'd get to them all anyway. It was just a matter of where to start.

Fletcher gave Shlomo a winning smile. Shlomo frowned.

"I've been meaning to talk to you about this stupid smiling thing," he said.

After a year of his mysterious illness, they put Fletcher in a hospital for a few weeks. But he seemed to get worse, so they sent him home again. They tried some medicines—some real ones and some pretend ones, just in case he was faking it. None of them made the slightest difference.

Then, after two years, when he could do little more than lie in bed, think of faraway places, and imagine packing his bags, suddenly Fletcher started to get better. It took most of a year. His appetite came back. His colour came back. The only thing he didn't get back was the three years his mysterious illness had stolen from him.

By the time Fletcher returned to school, he was twelve, although he looked nine. But he was smart and he'd studied at home while he was sick, so they put him in the sixth grade.

But before he went back to school, the medical people decided that, since he was fine now, it might be good to do that exploratory operation they hadn't been able to do earlier when he had been too weak. So they opened him up.

And what they found was a battlefield.

That's how the head surgeon described it. The inside of Fletcher's abdomen was like a scarred battlefield. Fletcher thought of his guts now as a place covered with empty helmets and wrecked swords and shields, all the size of Playmobil stuff but not in primary colours. Rusty. Stained. Whatever had been in him was gone, driven away by the soldiers of Fletcher's own inner power. That's how the head surgeon put it.

So it wasn't that Fletcher had no immunities. He had *amazing* immunities! His immunities had taken on something pretty terrible and licked it on the battlefield of his abdominal cavity.

As he was convalescing from the operation, Fletcher enjoyed thinking about his amazing immunities. It was nice to have a talent. In between worrying about going to a new school with kids he hadn't seen much of in three years and who looked three years older than him, he liked thinking about those Soldiers of His Own Inner Power.

Fletcher didn't hate school, but it was a little difficult to cope with after lying around dying for three years. But he was alive and that was so much better than the alternative. So he smiled a lot at school. He smiled at his desk, at his homework assignment, at his classmates. He even smiled at the soup in the cafeteria—even when it was green.

Some people thought he was cuckoo. Some people thought he really was nine and that he was a genius.

One person wanted to smash his face in with a brick.

That's what Ted Sawchuk said. "You wanna get your face smashed in with a brick?" He said it, Shlomo explained later, because Fletcher had smiled at Vivian Weir, who Ted considered to be his girl.

"You've got to watch that, Fletch," Shlomo said. Fletcher couldn't quite figure out what it was he was supposed to watch. He'd missed some of this stuff while he was dying.

The incident with Ted had been two weeks ago. Today as they walked to school with Fletcher feeling all those prickly places under his shirt, Shlomo tried to explain to him again about how much people like Ted hated people with winning smiles.

That wasn't Fletcher's only problem this morning. He realized that maybe the exotic place names all over his body might better have been a weekend thing to do. They itched, but if he scratched, it would be an unfair advantage to a place that didn't itch. He looked uncomfortable. The teacher noticed and asked him if he was all right. The teacher looked frightened and annoyed at the same time, like someone who didn't want a kid dying in his classroom.

Fletcher lost Anchorage and Reykjavik at recess, which made up for losing the hot places in bed. Shlomo hurriedly picked up any bits of paper near his friend in case anybody noticed.

"I feel a bit like a leper," said Fletcher.

"Like a leopard?" Shlomo asked.

"No," said Fletcher. "A leper. When bits of your skin fall off. Your nose, an ear."

Shlomo shivered. "Here!" he said and shoved the bit of paper with Reykjavik written on it into Fletcher's pocket.

Just then Ted passed by and glared at Fletcher. Fletcher smiled back.

Ted snarled but kept moving.

"I told you not to do that," said Shlomo.

"I can't help it," said Fletcher.

Vivian Weir was in music class with Fletcher. Ted wasn't. Fletcher tried not to smile at her. This only made things worse, because he looked like he was holding in a big joke. Vivian had never seemed to mind him smiling in her direction, but now she wasn't sure if he was laughing at her. She hid her face behind her saxophone.

It wasn't until the next day after school that Ted caught up with Fletcher in the hall. He jostled him heavily into the wall. The lockers groaned. As Fletcher got up, a piece of paper slipped out of his shirt and helicoptered to the floor like a maple key. Fletcher reached for it, but Ted put his fat, black boot on the slip of paper.

"Some of your brains fell out," he said as he bent to pick up the paper from under his shoe. It was stuck to a piece of chewing gum and he couldn't read it. The chewing gum made him mad, as if Fletcher was responsible for where he walked.

"He wouldn't have been able to read it anyway," said Shlomo later.

"How goes the battle?" said Fletcher's father. He was standing at Fletcher's bedroom door. Fletcher was stripped to the waist examining himself in the mirror over his dresser. Shlomo was lying on the bed reading Calvin and Hobbes.

"Only five places left," said Shlomo proudly, as if Fletcher was a show horse and he was its trainer.

"So I see," said Fletcher's father. But Fletcher could see in the mirror that his father's eyes were staring at the scar left from the exploratory surgery. Fletcher rubbed it gently with his finger, careful not to touch the exotic place that was closest to it.

"Does it still itch?" his father asked, kneeling on the floor to look more closely.

"Only sometimes," said Fletcher.

Shlomo crawled over to take a closer look himself. "Tashkent," he said. "Where's that?"

"In the republic of Uzbek," said Fletcher. "In the foothills of the Tien Shan Mountains."

"Get out!" said Shlomo, grinning. "Why couldn't you just memorize batting averages?"

"And if Tashkent wins," said Fletcher's father, "you'll actually go there?"

Fletcher smiled at the three faces in the mirror. "Don't worry," he said. "I'll write."

Only the city of Sofia fell that night, so Fletcher entered the schoolyard Thursday morning with four contenders left. Four corners of the world. Four places that were as yet only names and a few odd facts to him but would one day be strong smells and handsome faces and clanging noises that he had never heard before.

Someone pushed by him when the bell rang and dislodged Kowloon. And in setting up the screen for a movie about teeth, he jabbed himself and lost Rangoon.

Shlomo could hardly contain himself over lunch. "Let me see. Are they still there?"

And Fletcher would stare down the inside of his sweater at the two finalists and say, "Yes, they're still there."

Shlomo was acting like a drake honking around the nest where two eggs were about to hatch. Fletcher was pretty excited himself. Too excited to remember *not* to smile at Vivian Weir when she passed by his table with her lunch tray. She smiled back. She had a pretty winning smile herself.

Then he and Shlomo went out to the school-yard, and Ted was on them like a ton of bricks.

"Some guys never learn," he said, pushing Fletcher and heaving him backwards into the dirt so hard that Fletcher's hand smashed against a rock and got badly scraped. He ended up in that hard place where the playground ends and the fence begins.

"He's hurt," said one of the people who gathered around. A girl dropped Fletcher a Kleenex.

Shlomo didn't stop to think about it. He just started punching Ted, forgetting all about how big Ted was. "The guy almost died," he said. "Why don't you pick on someone who didn't almost die."

Ted pushed Shlomo off. "Because," he said, "if people almost die they should be more careful who they smile at when they start living again."

Fletcher dabbed at his hand. The Kleenex was soaked. He looked at Vivian through the crowd. He tried to tell her in that complicated language of facial muscles going every which way at the same time that he liked to smile, that he liked to smile at her, but that it didn't mean anything. And if it did, what of it, because it was only a way of being nervous and happy to be alive all jumbled up into a thing the face did without having to say anything.

Fletcher tried to tell Vivian with his face that he was going to travel to faraway places where smiling winningly might be the only form of communication left, and that he was practising on people with whom more advanced forms of communication like talking or joking around were out of the question, being that he looked like a nine-year-old among a forest of twelve-year-olds.

He tried to say something like that. Vivian nodded. She looked pretty confused, but she seemed to understand.

Meanwhile, the crowd around Ted and Fletcher was talking. They weren't generally pleased with Ted. "Leave the guy alone," somebody said. "He's just a little cuckoo."

"Cuckoo? Fletcher's a genius!" said someone else.

And then Shlomo, who had recovered from being pushed and was just about to attack Ted again, turned to see how his friend was doing and saw a tiny strip of paper on the ground.

"All right!" he said, diving for it. On his knees he cleaned it off, smoothed it out. The crowd crowded nearer. People said things like "What is it?" "Did some more of his brain fall out?" and things like that.

Shlomo read, "Dar-something... Dar es-something ..."

"Dar es Salaam," said Fletcher. "Founded by the sultan of Zanzibar in 1866."

Then, with everyone looking really confused and kind of left out and Shlomo whooping with laughter, Fletcher pulled up his sweater to reveal the last place in the world left sticking to him: the first place in the world he would journey to when he was older. It was right next to his scar.

Of course. He was always so careful about that part of his body. There was a battlefield under there.

"What is this garbage?" said Ted. Reaching down, he ripped the last piece of paper off Fletcher's body. "Tashkent," he read. "Who's that, Clark's brother?"

Some people laughed. The crowd kind of eased up.

"It's in Uzbek," said Shlomo. "In the shadow

of the Tien Shan Mountains."

"Well, in the foothills, anyway," said Fletcher, laughing. The crowd laughed some more, too. Fletcher noticed Vivian laughing prettily. Ted was the only angry person around.

"So what's it doing sticking to you?" he said. "You get too close?" Some of Ted's friends har-har-harred which seemed to loosen a few of the angry knots in his face.

"Not yet," said Fletcher. "Here. Give me a hand." He said it directly to Ted, but Ted was holding Tashkent, so other hands helped Fletcher up from the ground. Somebody dusted him off.

Ted looked around. One of his friends shrugged. Ted shook his head, shrugged himself, and shoved the paper with Tashkent written on it at Fletcher. When Fletcher took it, Ted noticed his bleeding hand.

"You gonna die on us again?" he asked.

"Nope," said Fletcher. "I'm just going to travel far, far away."

▲ ▼ ▶ ▼ ▶ ▲ ▼ ▶ ▼ ▶ ▲ ▼ ▶ ▼ ▶ ▲ ▼ ▶ ▼ ▶

HOW SOME PLACES GOT THEIR NAMES

by Graham Rickard

There are some fascinating stories behind the names of places—exploration, injustices, natural disasters, heroism, and even tongue-twisters!

Zimbabwe

The origin of the ancient stone ruins in Mashonaland, Zimbabwe, is one of Africa's greatest mysteries. They were built in the Middle Ages with huge granite walls, centuries before any other stone buildings in southern Africa. They were probably built by Bantu people, but could have been constructed by early traders from Arabia or India. The name means "stone houses" and was adopted by the black African national movements who were fighting to overthrow the country's white government in the days when the country was called Rhodesia.

In 1980 Rhodesia became an independent nation, and its name was officially changed to Zimbabwe. The country's national fish-eagle emblem was taken from a carving found in the ancient ruins.

The Amazon River

In Greek legend, the Amazons were a band of female warriors who made slaves of their male prisoners.

In 1541 the Spanish explorer Francisco de Orellana was the first European to travel down the river, from the Andes Mountains to the Atlantic. He reported that he and his men were attacked by groups of fierce female warriors, and hence named the river "Amazonas." An alternative explanation is that the river's name derives from "amossona," an Indian word for "destroyer of boats," because navigation on the river is endangered by floods, rapids, and tidal waves.

The Amazon is the longest river in the world, at 6750 km. Its Atlantic estuary is 240 km wide, and it turns the sea water from salt to brackish for over 160 km from the shore.

Phoenix

In an ancient classical Greek legend, the phoenix was a magical bird, as large as an eagle, with scarlet and gold feathers. Only one phoenix existed at any one time, but each lived for at least 5000 years.

As it approached the end of its life, it set fire to its nest and was consumed in the flames, to be born again from its own ashes.

In 1867, Jack Swilling visited a dry, saucer-shaped valley near Arizona's Salt River and realized its potential for irrigation. His company dug canals, sowed crops, and created a settlement. Swilling's friend Darrel Duppa was impressed by some ancient Indian ruins near the site. He predicted that a new city would, like the phoenix, be born from the ruins of the old.

His prediction was correct. The town prospered, and became the capital of Arizona in 1889. The ancient ruins of La Cuidad are still to be seen at the centre of a modern city of 500 000 people.

Tasmania

The first European discoverer of this large island on Australia's south coast was the Dutch navigator Abel Tasman, in 1642. He named it Van Diemen's Land, after Anthony van Diemen, who was the governor general of the Dutch East Indies Company. He had no idea that it was an island, and neither did anyone else until 1798. The name lasted for 200 years, and the island became notorious as a British penal colony for transported criminals.

When the transportations ended in 1853, the island wanted to improve its status. It felt that "diemen" sounded too much like "demon."

Unofficially, the islanders were already using the name of Abel Tasman, in the poetic-sounding form of Tasmania.

The Dead Sea

The Dead Sea is not really a sea but a large inland lake. The River Jordan flows into it, and there is no outlet to the ocean. The water evaporates constantly in the great heat, leaving the salts behind. The lake's salt content is therefore so high that very little organic life can survive in its waters. That is why it is called the Dead Sea. Another effect of the high salt content is that the water is very buoyant. It is impossible for a swimmer to sink.

The Dead Sea is one of the world's most famous inland waters in history, and there are references to it dating back thousands of years. It lies partly in Israel and partly in Jordan. Both countries use it as a source of salt and as a popular holiday attraction.

Cape of Good Hope

For many years Portuguese sailors had been exploring the western coast of Africa. They had been penetrating further and further south in an attempt to find a sea route round the vast continent to India. At last, in 1487, Bartolomew Diaz was the first European to reach the southernmost point of the continent and sail round it into the Indian Ocean.

Diaz did not see the coast on his outward journey, but on the return journey he sailed through terrible storms before he finally sighted the tip of the continent. He therefore named it Cabo Tormentoso (Cape of Storms). However, King John of Portugal was worried that other explorers might be put off by this name, so he changed it to Cabo de Boa Esperanca—the Cape of Good Hope.

Diaz had good reason for his original name. Twelve years later he was drowned off the Cape when his ship went down in a storm.

Llanfairpwllgwyngyllgogerychwyrndrobwllllan-tysiliogogogoch

With 58 letters, this village in Anglesey, in North Wales, easily wins the title of the longest place name in Britain. Translated from Welsh, it means "St. Mary's Church in the hollow of the white hazel trees near the rapid whirlpool and the church of St. Tysilio near the red cave."

The official name only consists of the first 20 letters. However, during the 19th century, the name was extended to become the longest in Wales in order to attract tourists. It is often abbreviated to Llanfair P.G., but the full name was used on the platform sign when the railway station was reopened in 1973.

Welsh people count only 51 letters in the full name, because in the Welsh language "ll" and "ch" are single letters.

CANADIAN INDIAN
PLACE NAMES

Bella Bella, Bella Coola,
Athabaska, Iroquois;
Mesilinka, Osilinka,
Mississauga, Missisquois.
Chippewa, Chippawa,
Nottawasaga;
Malagash, Matchedash,
Shubenacadie;
Couchiching, Nipissing,
Scubenacadie.
Shickshock
Yahk
Quaw!

Meguido Zola

THE PLEASURE PERIPHERY
Tourism in the Developing World

from *The Real World*

What are the benefits, and the costs, of a thriving tourist trade?

Increasingly, countries in the Developing World have become popular as holiday destinations for Western tourists—so much so that those countries now account for around one-eighth of the industry. The countries concerned have generally been keen to promote tourism as a means of earning foreign exchange, of stimulating the local economy, and of providing employment.

But in recent years the tourist industry has come to be seen as, at best, a mixed blessing. People have begun to calculate the full costs and benefits of tourism—especially its often contradictory impact on local cultures, the natural environment, and the economy.

Tourism certainly creates jobs. Although the work is largely seasonal, local people are employed in hotels, shops, banks, restaurants, and bars, as taxi drivers, or as manufacturers of souvenirs. But if labour is in short supply, and wage rates in tourism are relatively high, other sectors of the economy can be deprived of their work force. Falling local agricultural production, for example, will reduce food exports and push up imports of foreign foods.

Countries must also bear the infrastructural costs of tourism. In order to attract visitors, they may have to improve their roads, water, and electricity supplies, and build airports close to resorts. Although some of these new facilities are also of benefit to local people, many only serve tourist areas.

Dependence on tourism also makes a country particularly vulnerable to changing demand. Tourists are notoriously fickle; this year's favoured resort may have gone out of fashion by next year. Political disturbances, natural disasters, and outbreaks of disease or food poisoning can devastate a local tourist industry. Fiji's military coup in 1987 caused a 70 percent drop in visitor arrivals, despite a vigorous international advertising campaign to restore consumer confidence.

The great scale and complex structure of the international tourist industry could now bring about the complete collapse of a country's tourist trade. Tour companies can make use of any number of countries, each offering "sun, sand, and surf," and standardized facilities. Switching vacationers from one country to another presents little difficulty for the company, and may make no difference to the tourist, but is a disaster for the country that is out of favour.

The effects of tourism on local culture and environment can be mixed. Tourism may help to sustain native ceremonies and arts and crafts. Similarly, historic buildings and sites may be preserved, and sanctuaries created for wildlife. Yet tourism can also destroy. Native cultures can be debased, hotel developments may be unsightly, sewage and oil from boats often pollute beaches, and the breeding patterns of wild animals are disrupted. It is ironic that the very qualities that entice tourists to visit a particular country are those most threatened by their presence.

▲ ▼ ▶ ▼ ▲ ▼ ▶ ▼ ▲ ▼ ▶ ▼ ▲ ▼ ▶ ▼ ▲ ▶

PROBLEMS CAUSED BY TOURISM

- **St. Lucia:** When tourism developed, the island's balance of payments deteriorated as workers were drawn from banana production.

- **Fiji:** The military coup in 1987 caused a sudden drop in visitors of over 70 percent. Four out of five people involved in the industry were fired. The currency was devalued by 17 percent.

- **Seychelles:** Tourism has brought much-needed foreign currency but has led to soaring land prices and the disruption of fishing and farming.

- **India:** Hotel developments in Goa divert public resources from local people. Some water mains to hotels pass through villages without piped water.

- **Nepal:** The influx of hikers has worsened deforestation problems by increasing the demand for wood for fuel.

- **Turkey:** Tourist developments threaten the nesting beaches of sea turtles.

- **Venezuela:** Tourist agencies have used the powerful chemical dioxin to clear seaweed from beaches. The poison has killed millions of fish.

▲▼▶▼▶▲▼▶▼▶▲▼▶▼▶▲▼▶▼▶▶

TOUCH THE DRAGON
A Thai Journal

by Karen Connelly

At 17, Karen Connelly longed to experience a different way of life. Thanks to an exchange program, she left Calgary, Alberta, to live for a year in Denchai, a small farming community in northern Thailand. The journal she kept eventually became a book, *Touch the Dragon*. Here are excerpts from Karen's first three months in the country.

August 27

Nareerat is in the centre of Prae. The school has almost three thousand students, only five hundred of them boys. "It has taken a long time," says Ajahn Champa, "to integrate boys with girls." She is the head of the English department and speaks the language beautifully; it's the first real English I've heard since Japan, and I bask in the familiar sounds. She studied on scholarship in Australia and Britain, and exudes the wisdom of age and experience. Also the scent of lemons. She is spot-lessly clean and does not seem to sweat. A drop of salt water regularly gathers at my chin and slides down my neck as if there were a hole in my jaw, but Ajahn Champa's skin is dry and pale gold.

She sits down at the long row of tables in the English room and begins to tell me very matter-of-factly what I need to know. As she speaks, fanning her hand open and shut for emphasis, I realize this woman will be my greatest help. She can talk with grace about anything.

—The children in Nareerat and many of the townspeople will be curious about me; except for the occasional tourist, missionary, or Peace Corps member, white people do not appear in Prae. "You may get tired of all the attention, but try not to get upset. They only want to know you."

—I must not touch anyone's head, which is a holy part of the body for Buddhists. "And try to keep your head on a lower level than that of your elders, especially grandparents, for this is a sign of respect. You will make many mistakes at first, but that is all right. Thais are very tolerant people. But if you make the same mistake over and over, they will think you are very stupid or trying to insult them, so be careful."

—As the head is holy, the feet are unholy, and I have to walk around, not over, objects. It is considered rude to move and touch things or people with your feet. This explains why Meh got all flustered when I pushed the fridge door shut with my toes.

I spend my first day at school with Ajahn Champa. "The seamstress will have your uniform ready in two days. It causes quite an upset to have a student without a uniform." She notices the expression on my face. "Yes, I know, you do not like uniforms, but wait and see. You will soon realize that you are different enough, even in a uniform. It will make you feel much more Thai than you think. If you do not wear a uniform, you will stand out too much, and the students will not treat you the same as they treat each other." Already children appear at the doors, giggling. When they see me walking across the schoolyard, they wave and call, *"Falang, falang*[1]." Ajahn Champa says, "Once they get used to you and know your name, they won't do that anymore. They will talk to you." Before our serious, gentle conversation finishes, she asks me, "Which place is like a dream now, this country or your own?" I'm surprised by her question because it so closely touches my own thoughts. "My own," I say, "though Thailand was a dream until last week."

August 29

Food is extremely important; the people are insulted if you refuse to eat with them. Sharing is a part of friendship. No matter what it looks like, I try a bit of whatever is offered and just don't ask what I'm eating. I haven't encountered much to throw me, except for the spices. The food is delicious—

fried or boiled vegetables, chicken, fish, noodles, everything served with rice and sauces.

Ajahn Champa says the funniest thing on earth is watching a queasy *falang* trying to eat *goong den*, dancing shrimp. The tiny live shrimp are tossed into a bowl in the centre of the table, then doused quickly with a hot shower of spices. The spices poison the creatures, make them leap, flick up in the bowl. While they're still dancing, everyone around the table plunges in with a spoon and eats them live. It is almost a game, trying to get the shrimp into your mouth before they jump off your spoon. She says if you get to them fast enough, you can feel them wriggling down your throat. I know I'm not ready for dancing shrimp (often translated in restaurants as "disco prawn"). I knew I'd have to give up vegetarianism to live in Thailand, but I doubt I'll ever be able to put disco prawns in my mouth. Ajahn Champa says there is no fresher way to eat your seafood.

October 14

In the rose garden at home, we have a beautiful, leather-coloured lizard striped chocolate brown, his head like the long, sloped skull of a snake. He is a fat lizard accustomed to the luxury of enormous and frequent meals. The butterflies here have wingspans as wide as my hands; the dragonflies are so heavy they seem to fly slower than Canadian dragonflies. Everything is oversized and must be easier to catch for the reptiles. (This is probably untrue, but it sounds good.) … So much is alive, so much sings, crawls, clambers. I'm shouted at by the world itself.

October 20

The natural grace of the Thai makes my dancing class pure hell. Imagine a gorilla doing ballet. Imagine an enormous white chicken in red diapers. This is Karen learning classical Thai dance. I am with the youngest, smallest girls in Nareerat, the beginners. Beside them, I am monstrous. We wear baggy red wrap-pants (they really do look like longish diapers) and the string on my pants always gets knotted by the end of the hour class.

November 21

In Thailand, the sun has set: the earth arches into darkness and Canada rises to a cold morning. The sky here is orange and purple, an absent-minded blue. The first stars glow; no, they are so big they must be planets. I write in shadow, high on the terrace of the abandoned school. Ten metres away a stray cat gnaws a mouse. The first night mist uncurls in the valley. I'm trying not to breathe too loudly. Cat: don't crunch the bones. No one knows where I am and I am, incredibly, alone.

I've been here for three months: what have I learned? I don't know enough, cannot. I must attempt the impossible: respect everything, judge nothing, keep my self-righteousness to myself. I will never own any of this country, but it already owns part of me. Life is clearer here. Even the language is more direct. I often dream in Thai now. I've finally arrived.

1. **falang:** a word used to refer to foreigners; also a green fruit

Festival Time!

▲ ▼ ▶ ▼ ▶ ▲ ▼ ▶ ▼ ▶ ▲ ▼ ▶ ▼ ▶ ▲ ▼ ▶ ▼ ▶ ▶

The Powwow Drum

Long black braids and silken shawls
Moving side by side where the eagle calls,
Answering the beat of the powwow drum
                       we come again
                       to dance again.

Hey-a, Hey-a, Hey-a, Hey-a, Hey!
Hey-a, Hey-a, Hey-a, Hey-a, Hey!

Leave the dusty cities far behind,
Meet our brothers of the country with one
     mind,
Travelling from the east, north, south and
     west
                       we come again
                       to dance again.

Hey-a, Hey-a, Hey-a, Hey-a, Hey!
Hey-a, Hey-a, Hey-a, Hey-a, Hey!

Watching close the feet of lightning fly,
Fancy dancers free underneath the sky,
Joining in the circle moving round and
    round
                  we come again
                  to dance again.

Hey-a, Hey-a, Hey-a, Hey-a, Hey!
Hey-a, Hey-a, Hey-a, Hey-a, Hey!

Women shining like the morning sun,
Children making rainbows as they laugh
    and run,
The old and young meeting like they did
    long ago,
                  we come again
                  to dance again.

Hey-a, Hey-a, Hey-a, Hey-a, Hey!
Hey-a, Hey-a, Hey-a, Hey-a, Hey!

David Campbell

▲ ▼ ▶ ▲ ▼ ▶ ▼ ▲ ▼ ▶ ▼ ▲ ▼ ▶ ▼ ▲ ▶

▲▶▼▲▶▼▶▼▲▶▼▶▼▲▶▼▶▶

BANG! BANG! IT'S TET!

by Karen Benoit

It's midnight in Ho Chi Minh City. Suddenly there's a loud explosion. It's the sound of fire-crackers—set off to celebrate Viet Nam's most important festival.

City Celebration

It started at midnight—with a huge BANG! Then, a rapid RAT-A-TAT-TAT, followed by sparks and bursts of colour. In seconds, the booming, crackling, and whiz-banging became deafening. Hai stared wide-eyed at the brilliant display and the immense crowd of people that filled the streets. Hai plugged his ears and grinned at his father and his brother, Ly. Viet Nam's largest feast, Tet Nguyen Dan, had begun, and the fireworks in Ho Chi Minh City, the capital, would continue until dawn.

The next day, however, things were quiet. The first day of Tet symbolizes the coming year, so people are careful not to argue or do anything to bring bad luck.

A Feast

Later that day, Hai's family feasted on soup, rice, noodles, pork, chicken, fruit, and special cakes: *Banh Trung*[1] and *Banh Day*[2].

Hai's family had spent the previous week preparing for Tet. They had bought new clothes. At the farmers' market, they had purchased peach-tree blossoms to decorate their home and special fruit for the feast: huge grapefruits and sweet, round watermelons. All the food was cooked ahead of time because no work is allowed during Tet.

For the next three days, Hai's family would celebrate, until city life returned to normal on the fourth day.

Country Festival

Many kilometres away, in the village of Xuan Thoi Thuong, Cú Tí was delighted by the modest display of homemade fireworks that proclaimed the beginning of the festival in his village.

But at dawn there was silence. Cú Tí lay awake, listening for the first sound. He hoped it wouldn't be a rooster, a sign that birds would eat their rice, leaving a poor harvest. The ox's lowing would mean hard work for the year ahead. "Woof woof!" Dogs barking—a good sign: his family would be protected from thieves.

Cú Tí got up and put on the new clothes his mother had made. They were slightly large, but that was the tradition. It showed that she wanted to see her children grow during the coming year.

Cú Tí bowed to his parents and said *"Chuc Mung Nam Moi"*[3] to each family member. His father gave Cú Tí and each of his sisters, Chin and Noi, a lucky red envelope with money inside.

For Cú Tí, it would be a quiet day of feasting and celebrating with his family, including relatives from the city.

Tomorrow, the village farmers would have a ceremony in the fields. The village leader would plough a strip of land. This gesture shows that people must pay special attention to the harvest and work hard again for the next year.

But for now, many farmers would relax and enjoy themselves, taking up to a month off to celebrate Tet.

1. *Banh Trung:* a square cake made of sticky rice stuffed with pork and mung beans and wrapped in banana leaves. It symbolizes the earth.

2. *Banh Day:* a round cake of sticky rice, symbolizing the sun

3. *"Chuc Mung Nam Moi":* a wish for the coming year

▲ ▶ ▼ ▶ ▲ ▼ ▶ ▼ ▶ ▲ ▼ ▶ ▼ ▶ ▲ ▼ ▶ ▼ ▶ ▶

CARNIVAL IN TRINIDAD

by Vashanti Rahaman

Dazzling costumes, the music of steel-band drums, and partying in the streets—it's Carnival time in Trinidad.

Come one, come all to Carnival in Trinidad! Follow the cry of "Mas, Mas, play Mas[1]!" You will hear the lively music of the steel bands and see thousands of joyful masqueraders dancing in the streets. And, sparkling in the bright Caribbean sunshine, there will be the most marvellous costumes you can imagine, elaborately decorated with tinsel, sequins, feathers, and glitter.

Carnival, as we know it in Trinidad, Tobago, and some of the other islands of the West Indies, originated as part of Easter traditions. To many Christians, the time before Easter is a special season for praying and doing penance[2]. This time, called Lent, begins on Ash Wednesday and lasts 40 days (excluding Sundays). Many people make sacrifices during Lent; children may give up candy and other sweets, for instance, and some people fast or give up eating meat.

Long ago in Europe, the days just before the solemn season of Lent became a time of feasting and merrymaking. These days became known as Carnival, from an Old Italian word, *carnelevare*— *carne* meaning flesh or meat, and *levare* meaning remove. So Carnival was a time for people to remove meat and other tempting delicacies from their houses. And what better way to remove them than to eat them!

Over time, the celebration of Carnival spread from people's houses into the streets. Since some people didn't want their friends and neighbours to know they had been out dancing and celebrating, they put on masks and costumes. Soon Carnival became a regular festival with fancy dress balls and costumed paraders. When French and Spanish colonists came to Trinidad during the 1600s and 1700s, they brought their Carnival customs with them. The Europeans also brought slaves from Africa and, later, indentured workers[3] from India and China. So Carnival celebrations gradually came to reflect a blend of European, African, Indian, and Chinese music, art, and skill.

Today, Carnival in Trinidad is a very organized affair, with a national committee overseeing the celebrations. Although there are still people who make their own costumes and dance in the streets by themselves or with a few friends, most of the masqueraders parade in organized Carnival Bands, also called Masquerade or Mas Bands.

Anyone can try to organize a Carnival Band, but it is hard work. It can take almost a year to get a Band ready for Carnival.

The Band leaders choose the theme for their Bands and design the costumes. Although Bands may keep their designs secret until Carnival, most display drawings for their costumes at their headquarters, which may be a warehouse or just an empty lot covered with makeshift sheds. Some costume designs are even published in the newspapers. People who want to "play Mas" can examine the designs and then choose a Band. Anyone who can afford the costume can join.

Carnival Bands can have all kinds of themes. Some Bands represent different cultures or events in history, or even ideas like war and peace and happiness. The Bands are divided into sections, each section made up of masqueraders wearing the same kind of costume. In a Band called "Insect World," for instance, there might be sections of people dressed as flowers, bees, ants, and butterflies—or even a section with people masquerading as cans of insecticide!

Bands can have hundreds or even thousands of dancers, and the larger Bands may have dozens of sections. The masqueraders with the largest or fanciest costumes in the section lead the way, and the most magnificently dressed of the section leaders become the King and Queen of the whole Mas Band.

In the two weeks before Carnival, there are

shows in which the Kings and Queens from all the different Bands compete for the title of King and Queen of Carnival. The musicians who write, sing, and play the calypsos—the songs of Carnival—also compete with each other. Calypsos have a strong, rhythmic beat, and the lyrics often poke fun at things that people do, or make amusing comments on local or world events.

On the days of Carnival, some of the Carnival Bands are accompanied by steel bands with a hundred or more players. Steel band drums are made from oil barrels that are cut to different lengths to produce drums with high and low tones. Bumps are hammered into the top of each barrel to get a range of notes. With good tuners and players, a steel band can play almost anything a full orchestra can. Other Carnival Bands have music trucks, which carry a small steel or brass band or blast out recorded music.

Children in Trinidad join in the Carnival celebrations, too. There are national costume and calypso competitions for children, and many schools have their own Carnival parades. Sometimes each class in a school will design and make costumes for its own miniature Mas Band.

Carnival officially stops when Lent starts. The drums are silenced and the dancers go home. The beautiful costumes, which may have cost hundreds or even thousands of dollars, are thrown away or abandoned on street corners. Carnival in Trinidad, a glorious celebration of life and creativity, dies on

Ash Wednesday. But it will come to life again next year, dressed in new costumes and dancing to new songs.

1. **Mas:** short for "masquerade," a costumed celebration
2. **doing penance:** saying prayers or performing acts of kindness to show you are sorry for doing something wrong
3. **indentured workers:** people who agreed to work for others for a certain number of years, often in return for passage to the United States

▲▼▼▲▼▶▼▲▼▶▼▲▼▶▼▲▼▶▼▲▶▶

TARMA

by María Rosa Fort

Translated by Lori M. Carlson
and Cynthia L. Ventura

Martina and Julian are two children living in
Peru's capital, Lima, on the west coast of
South America. In this story, they travel with
their uncle to a village high up in the Andes
Mountains to celebrate Easter.

One afternoon late in April, which is autumn in
Peru, Julian and his sister Martina were looking out
at Lima's empty beaches. The wind idly blew the
striped tents where, earlier in the summer, everyone changed into bathing suits, ran into the ocean,
and dove into the cool and salty waters of the
Pacific. Now the water was grey, empty, and
uninviting. They could see the empty shores, the
waves beating down tirelessly on the dark sand.
"How many waves can the ocean have?" asked
Julian. "How old can the ocean be?" Martina
wondered.

Martina and Julian guessed at the years and

counted the waves, but just when they thought they had an answer, they realized they could still hear their watches ticking and see new waves crashing on the beach. The waves seemed endless and they couldn't imagine a city without an ocean.

That afternoon Uncle Marcelo came by to pick them up from their parents' house and take them far away to spend the Easter holidays in Tarma, the small town where he had grown up. "It's up there," he said, pointing to the mountains, "way up there, higher than the city cliffs and taller than the tall buildings that line the downtown avenues." Worried that it would be a long, cold drive, Julian and Martina bundled up under layers of woollen clothes and huddled comfortably in their uncle's old car. Each chose a favourite window in the back seat and waited impatiently for the hoarse sounds of the engine to pull them out of their neighbourhood streets, out of the humidity that already announced the coming winter. It was late when they finally left Lima. Martina secretly asked the sun to set later than usual so they could drive safely up the mountains and enjoy the new sights along the way.

They soon left behind the familiar city streets. Now, outside their windows, the pale walls of suburban houses started to disappear and the dust that covered everything in Lima was replaced by rocky formations of all sizes. Suddenly, a sombre river appeared on one side of the narrow road and farther ahead a cluster of fragile straw houses that seemed to bend under the weight of their television antennas. At the edge of the road, a boy with a stick in his hand was running after a skinny dog. Bushes and trees arched over the dry earth. Then Julian and Martina started to feel the mountains rise, growing steeper every minute. Soon the tall peaks enveloped them. Like a persistent worm, the car climbed the winding road up the Andes. Julian looked back and saw only mountains, more mountains, and valleys ending in darkness. The ocean was no longer there. It belonged to another world, and so did they.

Time went by slowly and they seemed to be alone on the barren soil of the Andes. Every once in a while a car or a truck would pass them, or an isolated walker would be seen steadily heading toward some hidden village behind the mountains. But for most of the drive, Uncle Marcelo's car seemed to be the only life on the silent mountains.

They finally reached the highest point on the road, where it felt as though they were at the edge of the sky, and here Martina started having the symptoms of the feared *soroche,* or altitude sickness. Julian quickly stuck some newspapers under her clothes, covering her chest with them, as his mother had suggested. Lying down in the back seat of the car, she breathed in deeply and waited for her body to get used to the dry, thin air of the Andes. The night wasn't friendly either. Darkness had set in, punctual as usual. But when the little town finally appeared in a ravine on the other side of the mountain, it was sprinkled with tiny bright lights. Outlined by the festive bulbs were the profiles of the people of Tarma curiously examining the many strangers visiting for Holy Week.

Tarma had been invaded. Lodgings proudly displayed their no-vacancy signs. But Uncle Marcelo, Julian, and Martina soon noticed that all the private homes were open and lit, their owners unfailingly standing at the doors. It was an old tradition. Families opened their arms and houses to receive, for only a few coins, those travellers who had nowhere to spend the night. Rooms that had been closed forever were now open, forgotten beds were remade, or if need be, creaking straw mats were thrown on the floor.

Uncle Marcelo, Julian, and Martina found a place in the old house of a kind lady. The rooms were set around a stone patio. In one of them, Julian and Martina went to rest for the night. When they closed their eyes to sleep, Uncle Marcelo was still looking out the window at the town in which he was born.

Early the following morning, Julian and Martina stepped out to meet the sunny day. The clear light of the sierra surprised the two travellers, who were used to the grey sky of their city. They walked through the narrow, cobblestoned streets. As they arrived at the middle of the town square, they looked up beyond the tiled roofs of the Andean town at the openness of the sky, hills, and pastures. A strange silence came over them. But

Tarma soon filled up with people preparing for the main procession of Holy Week. And when they were met by their uncle, Julian and Martina joined in this mysterious ritual.

At dusk, Tarma's residents and visitors from far away gathered together in the town square to chat and stroll. They talked about the next day's main event, when the women and girls of Tarma would go to gather flowers of every imaginable colour. With their baskets full and their swollen aprons resting over their thickly layered skirts, they would return to the city to cover the streets with blossoms.

At sunrise the next morning the city was empty and quiet. Martina woke up early and, while everybody was still asleep, went downstairs to the patio. She crossed it, headed toward the big wooden door, and struggled to push it open. From the threshold she watched the deserted street as though she were waiting for somebody. A girl with a basket on her arm walked past her on the other side of the street. Martina followed her in silence for quite a while until they reached the end of the town, where the mountain range began. She followed her new friend down a lush green slope that ended in a gurgling stream surrounded by a bed of flowers. There they stopped. The two girls smiled at each other and knelt on the damp grass. Together they filled the basket with petals until not one more flower could fit in it. Only then could they start on their way back.

Toward noon, Tarma came to life when all the peasant girls returned from the fields with their baskets full of flowers. Bending over the uneven cobblestones of the streets, the girls began to cover them with the colourful petals. Martina watched attentively. She noticed how carefully each girl's hands covered the cobblestones with designs made up of petals of every colour. Uncle Marcelo had told her these were images of Holy Week. Soon the streets of Tarma were transformed. Petals in the shape of a llama, a quino tree, a snow-capped mountain, and even a Donald Duck figure filled the streets. The cobblestones were now covered with rugs that seemed to be made out of light and velvet where all the colours of the world blended together. Martina discovered an unexpected beauty. "Hands are magical," she thought.

Meanwhile, on the other side of the sea of flowers, Uncle Marcelo and Julian were looking for Martina. They asked the barber about her, they asked the fruit vendor, the kind lady of the house, and her neighbours. But it didn't occur to them to ask the girls who had gone to the fields to pick the flowers. They finally found Martina near the square looking at the peaceful, flowered streets.

Soon dusk was ready to fall upon the town. Uncle Marcelo, Julian, and Martina stayed together to watch the procession.

When the last rays of the sun flooded the central nave of the Cathedral, the leader of the procession gave a signal to the faithful gathered inside it. They bent their knees slightly to place on their shoulders the heavy wooden platform bearing the statue of Jesus. The members of the procession timed their steps to the rhythm of drumbeats and trumpets. Behind them the people of Tarma and the many visitors accompanied the sacred images on their slow journey through the town. As the people advanced, the delicate petals died one by one. Absorbed by the drama of the procession, Martina looked at the peasant girl's hands now folded in prayer.

For hours, while the green fields around Tarma darkened with the setting sun, the faithful continued to walk on the flowers of Tarma. The procession wound along the streets and then back inside the cathedral lit with the flickering of innumerable candles.

The celebrations were over. In the town that night, everyone dreamed quiet dreams while outside the wind swept away the last traces of the llama, the tree, the mountain, the duck. The house of the kind lady was now dark. Everybody was asleep. Across the room, Martina heard Julian breathing deeply. She closed her eyes, and when everything around her disappeared behind the smell of her alpaca blanket, she said goodbye to Tarma. As she fell asleep, she could already feel the slow whirl taking her down the tall mountains toward the foot of the Andes. And further, down to the ocean, where the waves still crashed on the dark sands of Lima.

OBON: A FAMILY REUNION

by Sandy Fox

Okinawa is one of many small islands in Japan. Every July, Okinawans, like other Japanese, honour their ancestors in a three-day festival called Obon.

In the heat of the seventh day of the seventh lunar month, Okinawans visit their family tombs. Entering the patio area, they greet their ancestors and invite them to join the family for Obon. Long stalks of sugar cane are placed by the tomb door for the ancestors to use as walking sticks on their journey.

As the first day of the celebration approaches, women cook special fish cakes, tempura (batter-coated fried vegetables or meat), seaweed, and sweetened rice cakes (*moocha*). On the evening of the 13th, a black incense (*sanko*) is taken outside the house. The family prays to the invited spirits, and the smoke from the incense guides the spirits to the house.

"It's a big party," Toshiko, a resident of

Kishaba, says. "Whole families and all the dead people come to the family house and have a party."

Food and drink are offered to the ancestors on the household shrine (*butsudan*). Set in a niche in the living-room wall, the shrine has three polished wooden steps. On the highest step rest the long, thin memorial tablets (*ihai*) with the ancestors' names written on them. The lower steps hold offerings: porridgelike rice mixed with meat pieces (*jushi*), fresh fruit, liquor (*sake*), tea, flowers, and incense.

The next day at each meal, food is offered to the ancestors. Family members spend the day talking to one another and to the dead. They may discuss problems with the ancestors and seek their advice. Extended family members visit from house to house.

Before entering the house, visitors ritually wash their feet and legs with a grass brush. Then they pray before the shrine for the health and safety of the family. Ancestor spirits (*seishin*) are asked to grant prosperity and good fortune in the coming year.

Eating, dancing, and singing last far into the night. "It's a party to make the ancestors happy," Toshiko explains. "I play the *samisen* [a three-stringed guitar] and sing." Businesses close, and no farm work is done.

The third day's lavish supper party (*ukui*) lets the spirits know that everything is fine and they are free to return to their tomb. After the feasting, but before midnight, the oldest family member guides the ancestors to the door with the black incense and offers them gifts to help them on the "other side." Special money (*uchikabi*) is burned, and the ashes are mixed with uncooked rice and sake. Other bundles hold pieces of sugar cane, pineapple, and orange. These offerings are placed at the front gate. There the family prays that the spirits will return safely to the tomb and come back next year. Then the most colourful part of Obon begins.

Young men and women join in Eisa dancing. Each village has its own special costume of colourful tunics, bright sashes, and streaming turbans. Most men wear white pants with black-and-white striped leggings. The women wear short, navy blue, printed kimonos with a vivid sash, and thongs on their feet.

The Eisa dancers parade through the streets accompanied by men singing in quavery voices and playing a tune in a minor key on the samisen. Leading dancers carry large red drums (*taiko*) strapped over the left hip. Others wave smaller tambourine-size drums. As they beat the drums with fat sticks, the sound echoes for miles.

The drummers keep perfect rhythm while swinging their sticks in high twists and dancing. The women follow with gentle hand and foot movements. At each home, they ask blessings of health and prosperity, collect the ancestors, and help guide them home.

Although there is merrymaking and feasting, Obon has a deeply religious side. The Shinto and Buddhist religions blend with ancient beliefs that spirits of all objects can influence the lives of the living. Ancestor spirits are among the strongest forces for good or evil a family can have. People believe that past family members are concerned with the lives of the living.

It is the duty of the living to inform the seishin of the daily problems and accomplishments of each member. The living also are expected to pray daily for the dead and to care for their burial site. In return, the ancestor spirits, who can affect nature and events, are obliged to assist their descendants with health and prosperity. In Japan, the living and the dead interact on a daily basis. At Obon, the Japanese joyously celebrate this special family relationship.

▲▼▶▼▲▼▶▼▲▼▶▼▲▼▶▼▲▶

THE DAY OF THE DEAD

by Elizabeth Silverthorne

The Day of the Dead is one of the most important fiestas in Mexico. The word fiesta means "feast." Food is important in all fiestas, which are religious festivals in Spanish-speaking countries.

For Mexicans, death is a part of life. It is not something to be quickly covered over or hidden. In ancient times the Indians held a month-long festival of Death and Flowers as a reminder of the beauty and fleeting nature of life. The last day of their celebration fell on November 1. This was the same day as the Spanish festival called All Souls' Day, when the spirits of the dead were thought to return to Earth.

Today in Mexico *El Día de los Muertos*, the Day of the Dead, begins on October 31 and lasts through November 2. Weeks before the fiesta, markets are filled with toys related to death—cardboard skeletons that dance on strings, clay skulls, coffins with skeletons that pop out of them.

Families make careful preparations for the fiesta. They sweep and clean graves and tombstones. In their homes they set up altars with pictures of dead family members. Around these altars they place candles, flowers, and incense. The favourite foods of the dead are also placed near the altars.

Bakeries feature a special round cake called *pan de los muertos.* It may be decorated with different icings in the shape of a skull and crossbones. Sometimes the bread is baked in the shape of a man or a woman or a child to represent someone who has died. Children happily eat small blue and pink candy skulls that have their names pasted on the foreheads.

The Day of the Dead is a time to watch processions of marchers in skeleton masks and other costumes representing death. Sometimes groups of young men carry coffins from which fake skeletons pop up and wave playfully to the crowd. It is also a time to visit churches and pray for the dead.

Above all, the Day of the Dead is a time for families to visit cemeteries. They bring candles and food and armloads of *caléndulas* (marigolds), the special flower of the dead. They pile flowers over and around the freshly cleaned graves of loved ones. Petals are pulled off the marigolds and spread on the tombs in the form of crosses.

Families have picnics in the cemeteries. At night, hundreds of candles glow as families keep watch beside the decorated graves. Soft music from a mariachi band serenading the spirits of the dead may be heard in the background.

Although the Day of the Dead is a time to remember those who have gone, it is not an unhappy fiesta. Rather it is a time to connect the past and the future with the present. And it reassures those who are living that when they, too, have died, they will not be forgotten.

3

From Art to Architecture

▲ ▼ ▶ ▼ ▲ ▼ ▶ ▼ ▲ ▼ ▶ ▼ ▲ ▼ ▶ ▼ ▶ ▶

Ozymandias

I met a traveller from an antique land
Who said: Two vast and trunkless legs of
    stone
Stand in the desert. Near them on the
    sand,
Half sunk, a shatter'd visage lies, whose
    frown
And wrinkled lip and sneer of cold
    command
Tell that its sculptor well those passions
    read
Which yet survive, stamp'd on these
    lifeless things,
The hand that mock'd them and the heart
    that fed;

And on the pedestal these words appear:
"My name is Ozymandias, king of kings:
Look on my works, ye Mighty, and
    despair!"
Nothing beside remains. Round the decay
Of that colossal wreck, boundless and
    bare,
The lone and level sands stretch far away.

Percy Bysshe Shelley

▲ ▼ ▶ ◀ ▶ ▲ ▼ ▶ ◀ ▶ ▲ ▼ ▶ ◀ ▶ ▲ ▼ ▶ ◀ ▶ ▶

MARVELLOUS MONUMENTS

by Todd Mercer

In every corner of the globe, you'll find marvellous monuments, structures, and buildings that are a testament to human ingenuity and creativity. Here are the stories of five of them.

The Stone Heads of Easter Island

Like to try a little "head-hunting"? Then visit what has been called the most remote inhabited island in the world: Easter Island.

Easter Island is in the eastern part of the South Pacific Ocean. The nearest major island is 1900 km to the west. In the opposite direction, Chile, which governs Easter Island, is 3680 km away. The people who live on Easter Island—less than 2000 of them—are mostly of Polynesian descent.

The heads for "hunting" are the island's famous stone head statues called *moai* (pronounced "moe-eye"). About 800 of these statues, carved from soft, greyish or black volcanic rock, dot the coastline. Many face inland. No wonder visitors to Easter Island feel as if they are constantly being watched!

Moai are immense. Most of the statues measure between three and six metres tall, although a few stand more than nine metres in height and weigh over 60 t. About 60 *moai* are crowned with heavy red-stone topknots called *pukao*. Some of the *pukao* weigh as much as a couple of elephants (about six tonnes). Although some *moai* have toppled, others stand proudly upright, surveying the lonely landscape from ceremonial stone platforms called *ahu*.

Who created the *moai*? Recent research indicates that the largest statues were made anywhere from 400 to 1000 years ago by settlers from another Pacific island. The stone heads are thought to have been monuments erected to honour important chiefs after their death.

Moai were carved out of the slopes of an inactive volcano. The volcano is located inland on the eastern part of the island. Carvers used heavy stone picks to chip away at the soft, volcanic rock. About 400 unfinished *moai* remain at the Rano Raraku quarry—some still physically part of the volcano.

One of the great mysteries is how such large and incredibly heavy chunks of stone were transported from the quarry across rock-studded terrain to the coast—up to 30 km away! It would have taken enormous time and people-power. Some researchers believe the islanders used ropes to lower the completed *moai* from the quarry, and then placed them on log rollers. Another explanation suggests the statues were laid flat on Y-shaped wooden holders and hauled along the ground. Island legends provide a simpler explanation: the *moai* walked to their new homes.

The Great Wall of China

The Great Wall of China is probably the greatest construction project ever built. It is one of the few human-made structures on Earth that is visible from outer space.

Built to protect China's northern border, the Great Wall is 7400 km in length, including several branching walls. It stretches from the Bohai Sea (east of Beijing) to the Jiayuguan Pass at the western end of the Gobi Desert. Watchtowers rise above the wall every 100–200 m.

Where the wall passes through desert regions, it is often made of packed earth. But in the mountains, it consists of a double wall of stone blocks filled in with earth. Much of the wall is eight or nine metres high and over six metres wide, allowing enough room for horsemen to ride five abreast and troops to walk 10 abreast.

The first sections of the wall were built in the fifth century B.C.E. by various warring states. When Shi Huangdi became the first Emperor of a united

China, he ordered that the walls be joined together into one unbroken line. He wanted to protect Chinese civilization from northern invaders whom he considered barbarians. Beginning in 221 B.C.E., hundreds of thousands of soldiers and workers took 10 years to complete the Great Wall. Countless numbers lost their lives.

The wall continued to be expanded and rebuilt for centuries. But it failed to protect China when Genghis Khan's Mongol horsemen swept over it and captured Beijing in C.E. 1215. The Chinese rebuilt the wall during the Ming Dynasty (1368 to 1644), and most of what we can see today dates from this period.

Three sections of the Great Wall have been restored in modern times. Crowds of tourists each year visit the 320-km stretch near Beijing. It is an unforgettable experience to hike along the wall as it snakes up and down through impressive mountain scenery.

Machu Picchu, Peru

High up in the Andes Mountains of Peru lies a deserted, ancient Incan city, almost perfectly intact. Only in 1911 did it become known to Westerners, when American archaeologist Hiram Bingham discovered it.

Machu Picchu's location is breathtaking. The fortress town is perched like an eagle's nest in a secluded pass between two peaks, Machu Picchu

(Old Peak) and Huayna Picchu (Young Peak). Its hidden location kept it from being detected by the Spaniards when they invaded and conquered the Incan civilization almost 500 years ago.

Today, tourists reach the site by first taking a three-and-a-half-hour train ride from the town of Cuzco and then a 15-minute bus trip up a switchback mountain road. And visitors claim the trip is well worthwhile. Machu Picchu covers an area of 13 km^2 and sits on a series of 40 layered terraces. There are palaces, temples, a citadel, baths, and about 150 houses with steeply gabled or thatched roofs. An intricate system of fountains and canals once irrigated Incan crops. Everywhere there are steps—more than 3000 of them in terraced gardens in the area of the citadel alone.

In the centre of the city is the spectacular Temple of the Sun, built in a semicircle. Under the temple is the royal tomb whose entrance is guarded by an enormous stepped boulder.

The temple and other ancient buildings were constructed from white granite blocks, some of which are almost four metres long. In many buildings, the stone blocks are fitted together so perfectly that a knife blade cannot be inserted in the cracks!

Why was Machu Picchu built? Perhaps it was a refuge for Incan warriors from their enemies. More likely, it was a sacred place. To the Incas, heavenly bodies were gods, with the sun being the supreme deity. Ceremonies might have been held at the Temple of the Sun to commemorate the cycle of the seasons.

Since the Incas had no written language, we may never know for certain who lived at Machu Picchu, and when.

Venice, Italy

Say "Venice," and most people conjure up images of romantic gondolas on canals. Although the canals are its best-known feature, Venice is also home to some of the world's most famous art and architecture. In fact, the city is practically an open-air museum!

Venice is built on numerous islets and mud flats located near the centre of a crescent-shaped lagoon. Early Venetian planners used water to link the islets. The Grand Canal winds through the centre of Venice like an avenue. On either side of the Grand Canal, more than 200 smaller canals crisscross the city like streets and lanes. Crossing the canals is no problem, as Venice has about 400 bridges. Because cars are forbidden within the central city, people get around on foot, by water taxi or water bus, and on those beautiful (but expensive) gondolas.

In historic times, Venice was one of the great cities of Europe. It reached the height of its commercial and artistic power during the Renaissance. Many of Venice's most famous buildings and landmarks, such as the covered Bridge of Sighs, were built or added to at this time. Venetian artists, such as Titian, rivalled the artists of Rome. Venice also became a famous centre for music—the composer Vivaldi is one of the city's celebrated sons.

As glorious as Venice is, it is also extremely fragile. The city is slowly sinking on the soft earth of the lagoon bed. When high tides combine with certain strong winds, the lagoon waters rise, flooding the city. Heavy air pollution eats into the stone of Venice's buildings and damages works of art. As a result, in the mid-1960s UNESCO (United Nations Education, Scientific and Cultural Organization) started a worldwide campaign to harness the scientific and technical knowledge needed to save Venice. In 1988, testing began on barriers designed to prevent flooding of the city.

UNESCO also designated Venice a World Heritage Site. Not bad for a place that was once a lonely and desolate lagoon!

Petra, Jordan

You're invited to explore an ancient city built into a cliff.

The road to the city passes through the Sik, a narrow gorge in the semi-arid region of southwest Jordan. The Sik is about 3 km long, 100 m deep, and narrows in places to a width of barely 3 m. The gorge gradually opens out into a valley 45 km^2 in area, ringed by flat-topped mountains.

This is where you'll find Petra, whose name comes from the Greek word *petros,* meaning "rock."

Over 500 temples, palaces, and tombs are half-carved and half-constructed out of the spectacular pink sandstone cliffs. No wonder Petra is called the "rose-red city"!

Petra's architecture displays a blend of Oriental and Graeco-Roman styles. One of the most splendidly decorated buildings is the Treasury (el Khazneh). The façade (front) is a masterpiece of columns, mouldings, and crumbling statues of figures from classical mythology, such as Medusa heads and axe-wielding Amazons. Although called the Treasury, the building is actually the tomb of an early ruler, King Aretas IV.

Petra was built by the Nabataeans, an Arabic tribe who migrated from southern Arabia to the Middle East around the fourth century B.C.E. The tribe consisted of 10 000 nomadic Bedouins who traded between Arabia and the Mediterranean. Petra became the capital of their kingdom from the fourth century B.C.E. to the second century C.E.

Situated at the meeting point of two caravan routes, Petra was an important centre for trade in Nubian slaves, gold, and ivory, Arabian incense, Indian spices, and Chinese silk. With its own water source and protected by the surrounding cliffs, the city prospered.

Nabataean rule ended when Petra became part of the Roman Empire in C.E. 106. The city enjoyed a further period of prosperity until an alternative trade route developed.

A poster for an Indian movie

("Lights! Camera! Action! The Popular Indian Film," p. 73)

Costumed revellers celebrate Carnival in Port of Spain, Trinidad.

("Carnival in Trinidad," p. 44)

Venice, Italy

("Marvellous Monuments," p. 65)

The stone heads of Easter Island
("Marvellous Monuments," p. 65)

Two snake charmers in Karachi, Pakistan ("Music Around the World," p. 77)

A gamelan percussion orchestra in Bali, Indonesia. Notice the gong on the right.

("Music Around the World,"
p. 77)

A grocery market in Ho Chi Minh City is piled high with food as customers stock up on supplies for Tet, the Vietnamese new-year festival.

(*"Bang! Bang! It's Tet!"*, *p. 41*)

Machu Picchu,
in the Andes
Mountains of Peru

("*Marvellous
Monuments*," p. 65)

LIGHTS! CAMERA! ACTION!
THE POPULAR INDIAN FILM

by L. Somi Roy

India cranks out over 900 movies a year, making it the biggest film industry in the world.

Credit titles explode, and synthesizers, horns, and drums blast. The hero rants against food hoarders, breaks into a dance number with a beautiful heroine against a scenic backdrop, and scatters the villain's henchmen in a prolonged, bone-crunching fight. People in the audience cheer, whistle, shout out lines of dialogue, sing along, and even dance in the aisles. A typical popular Indian film is under way.

Three hours later, you are out in the hot, humid streets of an Indian city, with taxis blaring, bullock carts swerving, and jostling crowds of turbaned men, bejewelled women, and teenagers in blue jeans. All this takes place under three-storey-high movie posters with movie stars painted in toxic green, neon blue, and breathtaking magenta.

The blurbs scream, "Every Sinner Has to Pay the Price!"; "A Saga of Love Hate and Desire!"; and "He Sings, He Dances, He Kills, Too!"

India's film industry is the largest in the world, churning out more than 900 films a year—more than three times the number that Hollywood produces. Five billion tickets are sold every year to 300 million moviegoers in a country of more than 850 million people. As mass entertainment, it is unrivalled. Movie songs dominate the Indian music industry, and superstars such as Amitabh Bachhan, the hero of more than 90 films, make Arnold Schwarzenegger look pale in comparison. Some film stars, like Bachhan and the late M.G. Ramachandran, are elected to political office by adoring fans.

The typical Indian film is a star-studded affair. Each film has six or seven song-and-dance sequences and several fight sequences. Stories and themes are repeated film after film: good versus evil, the struggle of the poor, the sins of the big city, and the destruction of the family. These are arranged in separate scenes rather than straight forward plots as in Western films. The actors speak stylized dialogue accompanied and underscored by background music. The result is a heady mixture of fantasy and exaggerated realism that packs in the crowds. The biggest Indian blockbuster, *Sholay*, ran for five years in one theatre alone.

The Indian film industry also produces films by internationally known artists such as Satyajit

Ray, who was awarded a Lifetime Achievement Oscar in 1992 for his work. Many directors make artistic films, which are popular among smaller, specialized audiences.

In a country with many spoken languages, major film production centres in five different states make films in different languages. The all-India film is made in the Hindi language in Bombay, a city with eight million people. The other major languages for making films are Tamil, Malayalam, Telugu, Bengali, and Kannada. The country boasts more than 13 000 movie theatres, one-third of which tour, presenting films in outdoor tents. Tickets cost about 20 rupees (80 cents) in an air-conditioned theatre in Bombay and as little as two rupees in the villages.

Stars sign up to do 20 films at once. Superstar actresses like Sridevi work on up to six films a day in different shifts, shuttling from one studio to another. This schedule has earned them the name "taxi stars." An actress might start her day as a peasant girl, go to another studio and become a society lady, and end the day as a sweet, innocent young thing pining for her boyfriend. More than 600 film magazines cover the lives and careers of the stars.

The stars lipsynch songs sung by playback singers such as Lata Mangeshkar and Asha Bhosle, who are superstars in their own right, having recorded more than 25 000 songs each. Their songs are composed by hot music directors like Rahul

Dev Burman and Bappi Lahiri, and the lyrics are written by some of the country's finest poets such as Kaifi Azini. Sitars, synthesizers, pianos, and violins provide movie scores that move effortlessly from traditional Indian ragas to Mozart to hip-hop and rap. Music is critical in heightening the mood of a scene.

With the emergence of television and videos, watched at home or in video parlours across the country, Indian films are seen by an additional 200 million people. When the epic *The Ramayana* was broadcast on TV, the country came to a standstill as viewers tuned in. The 93 episodes of the Indian epic *The Mahabharata* drew 93 percent of all viewers, making it the most-watched TV series of all time.

The great Indian film bazaar is still growing, entertaining the masses as it has for 80 years. It reaches into all corners of the country with theatres, touring cinemas, videos, and now satellite TV.

MUSIC AROUND THE WORLD

by Robert D. San Souci

Music: it's the universal language, and it comes in all shapes and sizes. Here's a tantalizing tour around the world of sound.

All around the globe, people make music in countless ways for many different reasons. From singing *a cappella* (without an accompanying musical instrument) to a performance by a full symphony orchestra or opera company, music comes in many forms. From the first simple drums and flutes that date to the last Ice Age to today's computerized recording studio (where electronic synthesizers can re-create any sound from a plucked harp string to clashed cymbals), music has been a vital part of the human experience.

Sacred music, from the Gregorian chants of medieval times to Native drumming, enriches religious ceremonies. Music also is a universal means of artistic expression and celebrating special events; the key to deep relaxation; and a powerful way of bringing people together, even when they do not speak the same language or share the same cultural background.

*

In Pakistan and India, flute-playing snake charmers practise an age-old skill (see photo section). Such displays originally had religious significance, but today they serve primarily as a tourist attraction. In truth, the cobra has no ears and cannot hear the music. It is actually the rhythmic, side-to-side movements of the flutist that keep the snake mesmerized, or "charmed."

*

In Bolivia, any occasion is cause for a fiesta. Folk musicians help to celebrate the feast of the patron saint of a village in the Altiplano, a high plateau that extends from Peru to Argentina. They play drums and pipes made from hollow reeds that give their music a haunting quality. Because life is hard in this dry, windswept region, the musicians bring welcome relief from the people's daily labours.

*

Usually made up of 10 or so members, *gamelan* orchestras are a familiar sight in Indonesia (see photo section). The name comes from the Javanese word *gamel*, referring to a hammer similar to a blacksmith's. Most gamelian instruments are percussion—they sound when struck. These musicians play at private parties, public gatherings, even religious events such as a *bodelan*, a "birthday party" for a temple. Sometimes gamelans have huge gongs, up to three metres across, which hang from poles. Javanese legend says that a god invented the gamelan orchestra to summon other gods to his palace.

*

In Czechoslovakia, a father in a small town plays the accordion at a family party, while his young son tries to finger the keyboard. The child will have his work cut out for him if he hopes to become an accordionist. The accordion requires considerable practice, as players must press keys and buttons with both hands while pumping the bellows. It has been nicknamed the "squeeze box" or "belly pincher" because players hold it in front of them.

*

In Brooklyn, New York, the Pan Rebels Steel Orchestra captures the dynamic music of the steel bands that began in Trinidad and are popular throughout the West Indies. Traditionally, such instruments are made from the sawed-off tops of oil drums that have been hammered into shapes that produce different musical notes and "voices." These instruments provide the lively accompaniment to calypso songs.

▲ ▼ ▶ ▼ ▲ ▼ ▶ ▼ ▲ ▼ ▶ ▼ ▲ ▼ ▶ ▼ ▲ ▼ ▶ ▶

ARTISTS OF CANADA'S NORTH

by Lyn Hancock

There's something about the Far North that inspires the people who live there to communicate what they see and feel in a variety of creative ways.

One out of every six people in the Northwest Territories, and in some communities one out of every two or three, earn money by selling their art—an astonishing statistic.

Wherever you go in the Northwest Territories, you'll find people making things. Artists work inside their homes, on the step outside their doors, or in a shack on a street. They sell what they have created to visitors who come by, to the Northern Store, to the local co-op or, in a very few cases, directly to a gallery in the south.

Native artists and craftspeople have earned universal respect. Their works can be found all over the world in museums, art galleries, and private collections.

When you look at a sample of artwork from

the Northwest Territories, whether it's a small quillworked box or a monumental sculpture, you get a glimpse of the history, geography, and biology of a land, and the autobiography of a people. For Natives, art keeps their culture alive; in the words of one elder, it keeps *them* alive. It provides identity in a fast-changing world.

Below and Above the Tree Line

Dene and Métis, who live below the tree line, use porcupine quills, fish scales, moose and caribou hair, or beads to make velvet-backed pictures and to decorate clothing, jewellery, and birchbark baskets. They carve antler, horn, and soapstone, and make replicas of such traditional implements as skin drums, sleds, sinew and spruce snowshoes, and moosehide and bark canoes.

Inuvialuit and Inuit, who live above the tree line, carve animals, spirits, and scenes of traditional life from walrus ivory, whalebone, caribou antler, and stone. They make traditional games, tools, weapons, drums, and goggles from the same natural materials.

Natives now add metal, glass beads, marble, wool, and cotton thread to the already varied materials. They also employ new tools and techniques, such as weaving, printmaking, oil painting, and drilling with power tools. They make wall hangings in woven wool and appliquéd duffle; animal and human dolls of fur and duffle with leather or stone faces; duvets with silkscreened covers; and jewellery in baleen, sealskin, silver, and gold. Items from modern life, such as helicopters, oil drums, and Christian symbols, sometimes creep into scenes of traditional life.

From Parkas to Kamiks

Clothing is fun as well as functional. The North's long winters are brightened by the vivid colours and varied designs of parkas, jackets, mitts, hats, belts, and kamiks (boots). These can be made from furs, cotton, and other materials decorated with beads, braid, quills, hair, inlaid fur, or appliquéd wool. In the Northwest Territories, art is the stuff of life itself.

Different communities specialize in different things. Cape Dorset, the first northern community to gain international artistic recognition, became famous for its stone and marble sculptures and its print collection; Holman for its floral Mother Hubbard parkas with large "sunburst" fur hoods; Spence Bay, now Taloyoak, for its hand-dyed embroidered parkas and animal dolls with babies in their hoods; and Fort Liard for its birchbark baskets painstakingly decorated with porcupine quills.

Carvings represents 60 percent of all arts and crafts produced in the Northwest Territories, but with traditional supplies of serpentine and soapstone in short supply, the government now encourages its artists to use power tools to carve the abundant hard stone.

There are many Métis and non-Native painters in the Northwest Territories. Although not as well known internationally as Inuit carvers and printmakers, they record what is left of traditional life and communicate the North's special quality of light and space.

4

Ways
of the Wild

A Selection of Haiku

Red dragonfly on
my shoulder calls me his friend.
Autumn has arrived.

Sôseki

In storm-tossed grassland,
one leaf, one praying mantis,
tremble together.

Miyoshi

Detestable crow!
Today alone you please me—
black against the snow.

Bashô

Leaping flying-fish!
dancing for me and my boat
as I sail for home.

Kôson

▲ ▼ ▶ ▼ ▶ ▲ ▼ ▶ ▼ ▶ ▲ ▼ ▶ ▼ ▶ ▲ ▼ ▶ ▼ ▶ ▶

▲▼▶▼▶▲▼▶▼▶▲▼▶▼▶▲▼▶▼▶▲▼▶▼▶▶

GRIN AND BEAR IT
A Town's Un-fur-gettable
Neighbours

by John Grossmann

Come visit the "polar bear capital of the
world." You'll find a place where people and
wildlife live side by side in a unique setting.

The polar bear was coming towards us! This
wasn't a zoo. This was the bear's home ground—
the frozen land outside Churchill, Manitoba.

The bear approached slowly, and everyone
grew excited. A few dozen of us—polar bear
lovers from all over the world—awaited just this
moment. Cameras ready, we were warm (well, warm
enough) inside a special vehicle called a Tundra
Buggy. A Tundra Buggy has huge tires that don't
damage the delicate Arctic environment. They also
keep the buggy from getting stuck in snow or mud.
Through its big windows, people can see polar
bears—the huge and beautiful creatures the Inuit
named Nanuk.

Suddenly, the bear rose up on its hind legs

and placed its paws on the side of the Tundra Buggy. It peered in the window at us. Everybody cheered and cameras clicked pictures. When the bear lowered itself back down, there was a small wet circle on the window, where its nose had been.

Churchill is famous for such close encounters with polar bears. Located on the western shore of Hudson Bay, Churchill calls itself The Polar Bear Capital of the World. And it is. Every summer, hundreds of polar bears hang out near this small town. They swim ashore in late spring when the ice on the bay—their winter home—begins to melt and break apart.

Bear Necessities

Why do they come to Churchill? Because it's where the water first re-freezes in winter. The bears know they can cross the ice and get back to their seal-hunting grounds. In fact they can't wait to leave Churchill. By the time winter rolls around, they will have gone without eating for six months! (Bears live off fat stored in their bodies.)

The water around Churchill turns to ice around Halloween. That's when the bears begin gathering along the shore, patiently waiting for an Arctic cold front to blow in. It's also when scientists and tourists seem to outnumber the 1000 people who live in Churchill year-round.

Living with polar bears is a way of life for the townspeople of Churchill. Turn on the TV and a local cable station will remind you, "Remember, it's against the law to feed a bear." There's even a special telephone number to call if you see a great white roaming the town: BEAR 2327.

Lily McAuley raised six children in Churchill. She recalls hanging wash one summer in the backyard and seeing a bear headed for the front yard. That was where one of McAuley's babies was sleeping. Screaming, she ran to the front yard, grabbed her daughter, and rushed inside. Fortunately, the bear was probably as scared as she was. It wandered off without hurting anyone.

"You learn to become bear smart," McAuley says. She taught her kids to talk to themselves when they walked alone, or to make some kind of noise—you don't want to surprise a bear. McAuley also told her kids to do just the opposite of what most parents would advise their children. "Walk in the middle of the streets," she told them. That way they'd stay out in the open and away from bears.

Another person from Churchill, Dwight Allen, remembers running from a bear when he was about eight or nine. He ran right into a stranger's house! Allen learned early the warning signs of a bear about to attack. "If a polar bear hisses or blows out air, you run," he advises.

In Churchill, polar bears hunt through garbage cans and search through dumps. They might even wander down the main street. On Halloween night, people circle the town with cars. They turn on the cars' headlights to scare off bears.

That allows kids to trick-or-treat without worrying too much.

If they're not disturbed, polar bears usually don't attack humans. Still, since 1968, polar bears have killed two people in Churchill. In recent years, wildlife officials have set traps to catch bears close to town. They take captured bears to one of 21 holding cells in a building nicknamed the Polar Bear Jail. The bears are well taken care of, then released when Hudson Bay freezes over.

Tourists have been coming to Churchill to spot bears since the early 1980s. Scientists have been coming since the 1960s. Then, there were fears that polar bears were becoming extinct. So scientists wanted to study the polar bear population.

Bear Facts

No one is sure, but scientists believe there are from 20 000 to 40 000 polar bears in the northern Arctic. So they aren't an endangered species.

Although known by the nickname "great white," few, if any polar bears are pure white. Most appear off-white, or slightly yellow. Some even look light brown. This may be because they are related to brown bears.

Scientists believe that 100 000 to 200 000 years ago, brown bears may have taken to the ice in search of food. Over time, they developed lighter-coloured coats that let them blend in with their surroundings. Being white made it easier for bears to sneak up on seals and other Arctic animals.

Bear Care

After first putting them to sleep with a tranquilliz-ing dart, scientists have discovered a good deal about polar bears. For example, they can tell a bear's age by pulling a tooth and counting the growth lines—much as you can tell how old a tree is by counting the rings on a log. Some polar bears live to be 25 years old.

Scientists are very interested in the eating habits of polar bears. Full-grown males tip the scales in the range of 350 to 680 kg. Their layer of blubber, which helps keep them warm, can be as thick as 11 cm. They get this layer from eating the fat and skin of seals.

"We'd like to learn how the polar bear can put on so much weight and eat a diet so high in sat-urated fat and seem not to suffer ill health," says polar bear researcher Malcolm Ramsay.

Scientists also hope to learn more about how a polar bear can go for nearly a half year without eat-ing—and without hibernating, the way black bears do.

"This is amazing," says Ramsay. "Because if you or I decided to stop eating for so many months, within a short time our muscles would break down from lack of food and we'd be hospitalized."

Almost as incredible as a bear's appetite are its feet. A polar bear's feet are huge for its size. On land, they act like snowshoes. Some researchers are studying the bears' foot pads, or soles, for clues in designing better shoes for humans. In the water, these big feet work like flippers.

On water or land, polar bears are something to behold. Out the Tundra Buggy window, you can see mothers with cubs trailing behind. Sometimes the cubs sleep in a cute, furry tangle, using mom as a pillow.

Most exciting of all are the fights. Hungry male bears will circle a mother and cubs. The mother will hiss and run at the would-be attackers to defend her young. Bears also play-fight, as young bears stalk each other, wrestling and biting (but not too hard). It's their way of learning how to fight and of seeing who's strongest.

A good play-fight can last a half hour. Both bears get up on their hind legs for a clinch no human referee would break. When this happened on our Tundra Buggy trip, one woman couldn't resist saying, "That's what I call a *real* bear hug!"

TROUBLE IN PARADISE?

from *National Geographic World* magazine

The Caribbean country of Belize prizes its coral reef. Now danger threatens this national treasure.

From a distance you might mistake a coral reef for the crumbling, submerged ruins of an ancient highway. But come closer and you see a living garden—an underwater formation populated by a rainbow of brightly coloured marine creatures: bright-red sea stars ... green shellfish ... spotted moray eels. Schools of rainbow-coloured fish glide by. No wonder coral reefs have become favourite underwater playgrounds, attracting sightseers in snorkels or scuba gear.

Although a coral reef looks like a stony structure, it's actually a deposit left by tiny creatures called coral polyps. Each polyp is about the size of a pencil eraser, and has a soft body made up of a stomach, a mouth, and tentacles. The polyp deposits limestone at the base of its body. During the day it flattens itself against the limestone. At night it pops up and fishes for food with its tentacles. When the polyp dies, the limestone remains. Other polyps attach themselves to it and add their own limestone. Different groups, or colonies, of coral build different-shaped formations. Some formations look like trees, others like fans. As many generations of polyps live and die, the coral reef grows. Often it becomes a building platform for islands that birds, reptiles, and mammals claim for homes.

Like most rain forests, coral reefs grow in tropical areas of the world. Reefs take three forms. Fringing reefs attach themselves to coastlines. Atolls encircle mountains that break through the surface and then wear away. Barrier reefs form near the shore, separated from it by a narrow waterway called a lagoon.

The barrier reef off Belize stretches for 280 km along its Caribbean coast. Because it is largely untouched, the reef has become a laboratory for scientists. They can study it as it grows. They can watch the interaction of its various residents, and discover what cycles a healthy reef goes through, what damages it, and how long it takes to heal.

Although natural enemies such as coral-eating starfish can harm coral reefs, people cause the most serious damage. Divers and boats chip off chunks of reef. Pollution poisons polyps. Run-off fertilizer and sewage feed tiny plants called algae until they grow out of control and smother the coral. Warming water causes coral to turn white and die. Clearing vegetation on low-lying islands for pest control causes the islands to wash away.

The country of Belize has few natural resources. Turning its beaches into resort areas and blasting cruise-ship channels through the reef could help its economy. But Belize's citizens value their reef and want to protect it. They've already created a marine sanctuary, and have won a grant for protecting the entire coast. That means hope for reef inhabitants.

THE GOAT PATHS

I

The crooked paths
Go every way
Upon the hill
—They wind about
5 Through the heather,
In and out
Of a quiet
Sunniness.
And the goats,
10 Day after day,
Stray
In sunny
Quietness;
Cropping here,
15 And cropping there
—As they pause,
And turn,
And pass—

Now a bit
20 Of heather spray,
Now a mouthful
Of the grass.

II

In the deeper
Sunniness;
25 In the place
Where nothing stirs;
Quietly
In quietness;
In the quiet
30 Of the furze
They stand a while;
They dream;
They lie;
They stare
35 Upon the roving sky.

If you approach
They run away!
They will stare,
And stamp,
40 And bound,
With a sudden angry sound,
To the sunny
Quietude;
To crouch again,
45 Where nothing stirs,
In the quiet
Of the furze:

To crouch them down again,
And brood,
50 In the sunny
Solitude.

III
Were I but
As free
As they,
55 I would stray
Away
And brood;
I would beat
A hidden way,
60 Through the quiet
Heather spray,
To a sunny
Solitude.

And should you come
65 I'd run away!
I would make an angry sound,
I would stare,
And stamp,
And bound
70 To the deeper
Quietude;

To the place
Where nothing stirs
In the quiet
75   Of the furze.

IV
In the airy
Quietness
I would dream
As long as they:
80   Through the quiet
Sunniness,
I would stray

Away
And brood,
85   All among
The heather spray,
In a sunny,
Solitude.

—I would think
90   Until I found
Something
I can never find;
—Something

Lying
95 On the ground,
In the bottom
Of my mind.

James Stephens

TRAVELLING PESTS
Australia's Unwanted Guests

from *The Real World*

When a foreign plant or animal is introduced, by accident or design, to a country, sometimes the consequences are disastrous.

Until 1788, no plough or hoof had ever made its mark on Australian soils. There were no cereal crops, and no domesticated mammals (unless we count the half-wild dingo, introduced from India perhaps 8000 years before). There were also none of the common vermin (pests) that haunt the European, American, African, or Asian farmer.

European colonization ended this splendid isolation. Spurred by the urgent demand back home for products to feed and clothe exploding populations, the new arrivals converted vast areas of wilderness to agriculture. In less than a century, Australia was home to over 100 million sheep and around eight million cattle, far outpacing the number of people. Wheat crops covered huge areas in the south and southwest of the country, and great sugar cane plantations were established in Queensland.

The deserts of the interior demanded pack animals like burros and asses. Soon there were more camels in Australia than in the whole of Arabia. And along with the foreign crops and livestock came other alien species, including ornamental plants and game animals. Native kangaroos were too inquisitive to offer much in the way of hunting, so deer and even foxes were brought in.

Freed of nature's checks and balances, many alien species ran amuck. The prickly pear cactus spread like wildfire, soon covering millions of hectares. Rats and mice, which made their own way in ships' holds, multiplied at unprecedented rates. So did rabbits. With grass in superabundance, sandy soil for burrowing, and few natural predators, a single female rabbit can produce 25 offspring in one year. The Australian grasslands were overrun. Stripped of plant cover, precious soils were rapidly washed or blown away. Only in 1950, with the deliberate introduction from South America of the virulent disease myxomatosis, was the rabbit population finally brought under control.

For a few native species, like the larger kangaroos and the bush fly, the changed environment was a boon (the bush fly, for instance, found the abundance of moist cow dung very much to its liking). But having evolved over millions of years in the remote solitude of their island continent, most native animals were overwhelmed.

Driven off farmland by guns, snares, and traps, forced to compete for food and shelter, and exposed to predators like rats, cats, and foxes, they retreated to remote areas. Many vanished altogether. Of the marsupials—Australia's only native mammals—17 of the smaller species have already become extinct and another 29 are endangered.

But the migration of plants and animals has not been all one way. Australia, too, has been the source of transnational pests. For example, a colony of escaped wallabies has become a nuisance in Hawaii, and dense mats of the Australian swamp plant *Crassula helmsii*, originally introduced as an ornamental aquatic plant, are crowding out native water plants in Britain. Biologists fear there will be no way to halt the invasion. The biter has been bitten.

▲ ▼ ▶ ▼ ▲ ▼ ▶ ▼ ▲ ▼ ▶ ▼ ▲ ▼ ▶ ▼ ▲ ▶ ▼ ▲ ▶

TWO-WAY TRAFFIC

Deliberate or accidental, the introduction of plants and animals from country to country goes on around the world. Through misjudgment or mischance, many colonists have become serious pests, with few natural predators to keep their numbers down.

- **California:** Mediterranean fruit flies have caused hundreds of millions of dollars' worth of damage to the state's fruit industry.

- **Galápagos Islands:** The most destructive of the

archipelago's[1] unwelcome guests are goats and pigs. Goats strip leaves and bark, and compete for food with the giant tortoises and iguanas. Pigs uproot vegetation and dig for the eggs and young of birds and tortoises.

- **Hawaii:** The ornamental faya tree has escaped from gardens and is running wild on Hawaii and Maui. A rapid and vigorous grower, it crowds out native vegetation and spreads toxins through the soil.

- **New Zealand:** Rats, cats, ferrets, and dogs have had a drastic effect on New Zealand's wildlife, especially its flightless birds. In just six weeks in 1987, a dog released into a forest reserve killed 500 of the park's 900 kiwis.

- **Southeast Asia:** The South American water hyacinth—a vigorous aquatic plant—has spread throughout the tropics, clogging waterways and invading paddy fields.

1. **archipelago:** a group of many islands

▲▼▼▲▼▼▲▼▼▲▼▼▲▼▼▲▼▼

THE TREE LOVER

by Ruskin Bond

"One day the trees will move again," said Grandfather.

I was never able to get over the feeling that plants and trees loved Grandfather with as much tenderness as he loved them. I was sitting beside him on the verandah steps one morning, when I noticed the tendril of a creeping vine that was trailing near my feet. As we sat there, in the soft sunshine of a north Indian winter, I saw that the tendril was moving very slowly away from me and towards Grandfather. Twenty minutes later it had crossed the verandah step and was touching Grandfather's feet.

There is probably a scientific explanation for the plant's behaviour—something to do with light and warmth—but I like to think that it moved that way simply because it was fond of Grandfather. One felt like drawing close to him. Sometimes when I sat alone beneath a tree I would feel a little lonely or lost; but as soon as Grandfather joined me, the garden would become a happy place, the tree itself more friendly.

Grandfather had served many years in the Indian Forest Service, and so it was natural that he should know and understand and like trees. On his retirement from the Service, he had built a bungalow on the outskirts of Dehra, planting trees all round it: limes, mangoes, oranges, and guavas; also eucalyptus, jacaranda, and the Persian lilac. In the fertile Doon valley, plants and trees grew tall and strong.

There were other trees in the compound before the house was built, including an old peepul which had forced its way through the walls of an abandoned outhouse, knocking the bricks down with its vigorous growth. Peepul trees are great show-offs. Even when there is no breeze, their broad-chested, slim-waisted leaves will spin like tops, determined to attract your attention and invite you into the shade.

Grandmother had wanted the peepul tree cut down, but Grandfather had said, "Let it be. We can always build another outhouse."

The gardener, Dhuki, who was a Hindu, was pleased that we had allowed the tree to live. Peepul trees are sacred to Hindus, and some people believe that ghosts live in the branches.

"If we cut the tree down, wouldn't the ghosts go away?" I asked.

"I don't know," said Grandfather. "Perhaps they'd come into the house."

Dhuki wouldn't walk under the tree at night. He said that once, when he was a youth, he had wandered beneath a peepul tree late at night, and that something heavy had fallen with a thud on his shoulders. Since then he had always walked with a slight stoop, he explained.

"Nonsense," said Grandmother, who didn't believe in ghosts. "He got his stoop from squatting on his haunches year after year, weeding with that tiny spade of his!"

I never saw any ghosts in our peepul tree. There are peepul trees all over India, and people sometimes leave offerings of milk and flowers beneath them to keep the spirits happy. But since no one left any offerings under our tree, I expect the ghosts left in disgust, to look for peepul trees where there was both board and lodging.

Grandfather was about sixty, a lean active man who still rode his bicycle at great speed. He had stopped climbing trees a year previously, when he had got to the top of the jack-fruit tree and had been unable to come down again. We'd had to fetch a ladder for him.

Grandfather bathed quite often but got back into his gardening clothes immediately after the bath. During meals, ladybirds or caterpillars would sometimes walk off his shirt-sleeves and wander about on the tablecloth, and this always annoyed Grandmother.

She grumbled at Grandfather a lot, but he didn't mind, because he knew she loved him.

My favourite tree was the banyan which grew behind the house. Its spreading branches, which hung to the ground and took root again, formed a number of twisting passageways. The tree was older than the house, older than my grandparents; I could hide in its branches, behind a screen of thick green leaves, and spy on the world below.

The banyan tree was a world in itself, populated with small animals and large insects. While the leaves were still pink and tender, they would be visited by the delicate map butterfly, who left her eggs in their care. The "honey" on the leaves—a sweet, sticky smear—also attracted the little striped squirrels, who soon grew used to having me in the tree and became quite bold, accepting gram[1] from my hand.

At night the tree was visited by the hawk cuckoo. Its shrill nagging cry kept us awake on hot summer nights. Indians called the bird "Paos-ala," which means "Rain is coming!" But according to Grandfather, when the bird was in full cry it seemed to be shouting: "Oh dear, oh dear! How very hot it's getting! We feel it ... we feel it ... WE FEEL IT!"

Grandfather wasn't content with planting trees in our garden. During the rains we would walk into the jungle beyond the riverbed, armed with cuttings and saplings, and these we would plant in the forest, beside the tall Sal and Shisham trees.

"But no one ever comes here," I protested, the

first time we did this. "Who is going to see them?"

"We're not planting for people only," said Grandfather. "We're planting for the forest—and for the birds and animals who live here and need more food and shelter."

He told me how men, and not only birds and animals, needed trees—for keeping the desert away, for attracting rain, for preventing the banks of rivers from being washed away, and for wild plants and grasses to grow beneath.

"And for timber?" I asked, pointing to the Sal and Shisham trees.

"Yes, and for timber. But men are cutting down the trees without replacing them. For every tree that's felled, we must plant *two*. Otherwise, one day there'll be no forests at all, and the world will become one great desert."

The thought of a world without trees became a sort of nightmare for me—it's one reason why I shall never want to live on the treeless Moon—and I helped Grandfather in his tree-planting with even greater enthusiasm. He taught me a poem by George Morris, and we would recite it together:

> *Woodman, spare that tree!*
> *Touch not a single bough!*
> *In youth it sheltered me,*
> *And I'll protect it now.*

"One day the trees will move again," said Grandfather. "They've been standing still for thousands of years, but one day they'll move again. There was a time when trees could walk about like people, but along came the Devil and cast a spell over them, rooting them to one place. But they're always trying to move—see how they reach out with their arms!—and some of them, like the banyan tree with its travelling roots, manage to get quite far!"

In the autumn, Grandfather took me to the hills. The deodars (Indian cedars), oaks, chestnuts, and maples were very different from the trees I had grown up with in Dehra. The broad leaves of the horse chestnut had turned yellow, and smooth brown chestnuts lay scattered on the roads. Grandfather and I filled our pockets with them, then climbed the slope of a bare hill and started planting the chestnuts in the ground.

I don't know if they ever came up, because I never went there again. Goats and cattle grazed freely on the hill, and, if the trees did come up in the spring, they may well have been eaten; but I like to think that somewhere in the foothills of the Himalayas there is a grove of chestnut trees, and that birds and flying foxes and cicadas have made their homes in them.

Back in Dehra, we found an island, a small rocky island in the middle of a dry riverbed. It was one of those riverbeds, so common in the Doon valley, which are completely dry in summer but flooded during the monsoon rains. A small mango tree was growing in the middle of the island, and

Grandfather said, "If a mango can grow here, so can other trees."

As soon as the rains set in—and while the river could still be crossed—we set out with a number of tamarind, laburnum, and coral-tree saplings and cuttings, and spent the day planting them on the island.

When the monsoon set in, the trees appeared to be flourishing.

The monsoon season was the time for rambling about. At every turn there was something new to see. Out of earth and rock and leafless bough, the magic touch of the monsoon rains had brought life and greenness. You could almost see the broad-leaved vines grow. Plants sprang up in the most unlikely places. A peepul would take root in the ceiling, a mango would sprout on the windowsill. We did not like to remove them; but they had to go, if the house was to be kept from falling down.

"If you want to live in a tree, it's all right by me," said Grandmother. "But I like having a roof over my head, and I'm not going to have it brought down by the jungle!"

The common monsoon sights along the Indian roads were always picturesque—the wide plains, with great herds of smoke-coloured, delicate-limbed cattle being driven slowly home for the night, accompanied by several ungainly buffaloes, and flocks of goats and black long-tailed sheep. Then you came to a pond, where some buffaloes were enjoying themselves, with no part of them visible but the tips of their noses, while on their backs were a number of merry children, perfectly and happily naked.

The banyan tree really came to life during the monsoon, when the branches were thick with scarlet figs. Humans couldn't eat the berries, but the many birds that gathered in the tree—gossipy rosy pastors, quarrelsome mynahs, cheerful bulbuls and coppersmiths, and sometimes a noisy, bullying crow—feasted on them. And when night fell and the birds were resting, the dark flying foxes flapped heavily about the tree, chewing and munching loudly as they clambered over the branches.

The tree crickets were a band of willing artists who started their singing at almost any time of the day but preferably in the evenings. Delicate pale green creatures with transparent wings, they were hard to find amongst the lush monsoon foliage; but once found, a tap on the bush or leaf on which one of them sat would put an immediate end to its performance.

At the height of the monsoon, the banyan tree was like an orchestra with the musicians constantly turning up. Birds, insects, and squirrels welcomed the end of the hot weather and the cool quenching relief of the monsoon.

A toy flute in my hands, I would try adding my shrill piping to theirs. But they must have thought poorly of my piping, for, whenever I played, the birds and the insects kept a pained and puzzled silence.

I wonder if they missed me when I went away—for when the War came, followed by the Independence of India, I was sent to a boarding school in the hills. Grandfather's house was put up for sale. During the holidays I went to live with my parents in Delhi, and it was from them I learnt that my grandparents had gone to England.

When I finished school, I too went to England with my parents, and was away from India for several years.

But recently I was in Dehra again, and, after first visiting the old house—where I found that the banyan tree had grown over the wall and along part of the pavement, almost as though it had tried to follow Grandfather—I walked out of town towards the riverbed.

It was February, and, as I looked across the dry watercourse, my eye was caught by the spectacular red plumes of the coral blossom. In contrast with the dry riverbed, the island was a small green paradise. When I walked across to the trees, I noticed that a number of squirrels had come to live in them. And a koel (a sort of crow-pheasant) challenged me with a mellow "who-are-you, who-are-you…."

But the trees seemed to know me. They whispered among themselves and beckoned me nearer. And looking around, I noticed that other small trees and wild plants and grasses had sprung up under the protection of the trees we had placed there.

The trees had multiplied! They were moving. In one small corner of the world, Grandfather's dream was coming true, and the trees were moving again.

1. **gram:** the seeds of a mung bean or a chickpea plant

5

Homecoming

The Profile of Africa

We wear our skins like a fine fabric
we people of colour
brown black tan coffee coffee cream ebony
beautiful, strong, exotic in profile
flowering lips
silhouette obsidian planes, curves, structure
like a many-shaded mosaic
we wear our skin like a flag
we share our colour like a blanket
we cast our skin like a shadow
we wear our skin like a map
chart my beginning by my colour
chart my beginning by my profile
read the map of my heritage in
my face
my skin
the dark flash of eye
the profile of Africa.

Maxine Tynes

▲▼▶▼▶▲▼▶▼▶▲▼▶▼▶▲▼▶▼▶

▲▼▶▼▲▼▶▼▲▼▶▼▲▼▶▼▲▼▶▼

THE LION'S PAW

by Tepilit Ole Saitoti

In his memoir *The Worlds of a Maasai Warrior,* Tepilit Ole Saitoti describes his childhood growing up on the Serengeti plains in Africa. In this excerpt from the book, Saitoti has been away at school and has just returned home, in time to witness the celebration of Maasai warriors after a successful lion hunt.

At the end of 1965 I completed eighth grade at Longido Upper Primary School. When we graduated, most of the students were in tears, for we knew we might not see each other ever again. There were few secondary schools and only a limited number of students could be accommodated, only those who passed the entrance examination. My desire for more learning had been kindled, so at home I waited anxiously for a letter of acceptance, but none came. My life was once again like that of any Maasai youth. I tended cattle and grew tall enough to carry my father's spear. My father thought me useful because I could speak Kiswahili and was even able to communicate a little in English, the white people's language.

I heard stories about Maasai warriors, how brave and proud they were. They were honoured by my people. One who was brave could court the beautiful Maasai girls. They would dance and sing to him songs of conquest, lion hunting, beauty, sadness. I heard talk of the adventures of warriors; I was excited to hear about them confronting lions and enemies, but also a little afraid. Only good warriors were respected by my people, and I wondered if I would be able to do all the things a good warrior must do.

I had been thrilled by a ceremony I once saw performed when a lion was killed, and felt lucky that I was present, because I had missed out on so many traditional events while I was away at school.

It had been a clear day. I walked out of the house of one of my father's wives, scratched myself, and yawned lazily, staring in the direction of another house at the other side of the kraal[1]. I looked at the sun overhead and thought that the cattle would be resting under the shade of trees until it got cooler; then they would graze again. I wished I had been with the herd, because I was accustomed to tending them and found it boring to be idle at home.

About to enter another house in search of people to talk to, I heard some strange noises and listened intently. I saw two men on a nearby hill approaching, and running to greet them was a young girl. The warriors must have told her something, because in a matter of seconds she ran back excitedly to the village, passing women who were sewing beads, speaking rapidly to them, and running on, passing me without speaking, though I had called to her.

The women stood up and walked hurriedly toward their houses, and as they passed, one told me, "Warriors have killed a lion and we are going to prepare for the dance." I looked up the hill, but the two men had disappeared. I wanted to go after them, but was afraid they would not be pleased because warriors don't get along well with boys, for boys are always teasing the warriors' girls. But my curiosity would not let me stand still, so I kept walking up the hill cautiously.

Two girls followed me up the hill, running: the one who had passed me earlier and another, both elegantly dressed. They went by me smiling, and I smiled back, but they didn't say a word. I was taken by their beauty and I let them know it, but they only looked back at me and laughed.

I looked down at the kraal and saw a crowd forming. It amazed me how the news had spread as fast as grass fire, and I decided it would be better to join the crowd and wait for the warriors to arrive. When I joined the people, everyone was wondering whether I had any new information. As everyone stared at me I felt uncomfortable. I walked around to the back of the crowd. I saw everyone there—old and young—and thought, This must be a momentous occasion because old people are here. My sister came over to me and asked me whether I had seen the warriors, and I said no. She added, "They'll come soon because the girls have already gone to meet them." She said that she was pleased that I was there because it was a good experience for me. "These are high moments in the life of a Maasai man, and they are worth seeing. Today you will see something for the first time with your own eyes and tell stories to others."

The sound of bells ringing interrupted our conversation as warriors walked up the hill. Two warriors and two very well-dressed girls approached. I had never seen anything like it in all my sixteen years on earth! The ostrich feathers on their heads, the swinging tails on the tip of the first warrior's spear, the big paw on the second warrior's spear tip, their anointed bodies glittering in the hot sun, the girls' dresses full of different-coloured beads—all were breathtaking. Nearly everybody was well dressed except me and the boys of my age; the young girls had on their best. I was embarrassed and wanted to go and change, but it was too late. Anyway, I wasn't alone, so I waited and watched.

Both couples came forward one behind the other, moving to the same rhythm. Both warriors appeared taller than anyone else because of the ostrich feathers on their headdresses. Each held his girl by her little finger and carried a spear in the other hand. Bells tied to the thighs of the warriors and the regular chanting of the crowd played out a rhythm, as the kraal's best singer sang lyrically: he seemed to have the most melodious voice I had ever heard. The lions' tails stuck to the tip of one spear swung like whips in the air, and the paw on the tip of the other spear evoked the might of the beast. The couples danced backward and forward with style. All the spectators followed them and watched, giving the warriors and their partners enough room to move. The whole thing was hypnotic; we were all taken by the swinging of the tails and the moving from side to side of the ostrich feathers crowning the warriors' heads. Many of us even started dancing unawares.

Soon the dance stopped. The warriors went inside the houses for milk and then rested; then they came out again. We all danced to the ceremonial songs together; anyone who felt like it could. The old people watched and were pleased. The day went by very fast. We had to stop our celebrations when the herds were about to return to the kraal and it would be time to work again.

The elders blessed the two decorated warriors, telling them to remain brave and have long lives and always save people and cattle. Many people shook their hands and praised the warriors, who replied that they had done only what Maasai warriors were supposed to do. Everything was free for them and everyone liked them. I thought of

how proud they must have felt and how I would
have liked to be one of them and be able to court
one of the girls who had danced.

I watched as the warriors moved along into
the distance. This had been the last of the eight
kraals at which they had danced, and now by tradition they had to part with their ritual objects, the
tails and the paw. They hid them far away from our
kraal, in a place where they thought children
would never find them and against the direction of
the prevailing wind (the lion smell could disturb
the cattle).

I had followed the warriors to the hiding
place. I made sure they didn't see me. I wanted the
tails and the paw to dance with the next day when
my friends and I would go to take care of the herds.
When the warriors left, I ran to the tree where they
had been, and when I saw the tail close up, lying in
the grass, I was scared to death, thinking at first
that it was a python. But soon I saw the paw, too,
and breathed a sigh of relief. I touched the paw and
the tails and couldn't believe that lions were that
big, because I myself had never seen one. I noticed
that all the claws had been removed from the paw,
and I saw that it was practically all muscle and
hardly any bone, and only a little moisture where
marrow should have been. I wanted to hide my
newfound treasures in a safe place where hyenas
couldn't find them, so I decided to put them up on
the branch of a tree. Before I put the paw down, I
hefted it to see how much it weighed. I knew I had

been misled by people who had told me that a lion is the size of a donkey. When I came back the following morning to retrieve the ritual objects, they were gone.

1. **kraal:** a walled village found in many parts of eastern and southern Africa

HOMES ON THE MOVE

from *The Real World*

In many parts of the world there are groups of people whose homes are temporary, not permanent. These people, called nomads, move on when the seasons change or to search for new sources of food or water.

For most people, home and settlement remain fixed in space. But for some people they change daily, or with the seasons. A diminishing but significant number of societies still live as they have always done, hunting, fishing, and gathering, or herding animals.

Hunter-gatherer bands are generally around 30 strong. Any more, and the effort required to feed everybody is considered too great. Any fewer, and the social structure is weakened.

Yet such peoples are not "unsociable." On the contrary, periods when food is especially abundant are often taken as an opportunity to celebrate in large groups. The Ona of Tierra del Fuego[1], who generally spend their lives in tiny bands in a ceaseless search for shellfish, collect together whenever a whale is stranded. Likewise, the !Kung people of the Kalahari Desert in southern Africa gather in groups of a hundred or more when they kill a large animal such as a wildebeest or an eland. They may also collect together to share resources when these are particularly scarce, as during the winter dry period, when they congregate around the few permanent water holes.

Such gatherings are often associated with ceremonies and other collective projects—initiations, storytelling, healing, and the arrangement of marriages.

Why Nomads Move

The movements of nomads are not random. Most moves are related to the seasonal and longer-term availability of food, and the recognition of the customary rights of other groups to exploit the environment. In many cases, a lifetime's travel for a nomad means covering hundreds if not thousands of square kilometres.

Some journeys may be undertaken regularly every year. Many pastoral nomads drive their herds between traditional spring and winter pastures. Although the pastoral Kazaks of central Asia lead a wandering life for much of the year, each clan returns to its own customary territory for the winter.

Many hunter-gatherers leave areas "fallow"

for long periods, sometimes 20 or more years, before returning. If they are forced to return sooner, the subsequent supply of food is harmed because the land and its plants and animals have not had a chance to recuperate. Native peoples are on the whole much less destructive of a forest's or a desert's long-term, sustainable productivity than intruders without specialist knowledge of these fragile ecosystems.

A Disappearing Way of Life

In many parts of the world nomads are being forced for economic or political reasons to abandon traditional ways of life. In some cases lifestyles are adapted to modern circumstances. Groups of Fulani herders in Mali and northern Nigeria continue to supply beef in the area, but they have exchanged their former independence for regular waged employment. The Bedouin of the Arabian Desert, one-time camel caravaners, now dominate long-haul trucking.

But for other former wandering peoples who have been forced to settle, the experience has been psychologically and culturally devastating. The social structures that once bound them together are strained to breaking point. When the Chenchu hunters of Andhra Pradesh in India were forcibly settled, the incidence of violent crime among them rose alarmingly.

Some members of one-time mobile societies

are now attempting to turn back the clock to ensure their survival. Aboriginal Australians are returning to the traditional life, retracing the "song lines" established by their ancestors.

1. **Tierra del Fuego:** a group of islands forming the southern tip of South America

▲▼▶▼▶▲▼▶▼▶▲▼▶▼▶▲▼▶▼▶▲▼▶▼▶▶

NOMADIC DWELLINGS

North American Plains Indians traditionally lived in tepees made of buffalo skins—later canvas— stretched over poles of pine, cedar, or spruce.

The skin-over-wooden-frame style of tent is still used by the nomadic Chukchi people of the Siberian Arctic, but they use walrus skins.

The traditional igloos of the Inuit are made from blocks of compacted snow, laid in an ascending spiral so that the dome stands up without scaffolding. The exit tunnel is built with a right-angled bend to keep out blasts of cold air, and the main chamber is hung with skins. If several families are camping together, individual igloos may be joined by tunnels leading to a large chamber designed as a meeting place.

The yurta, or tent-huts, made by the Kazaks of central Asia may be 1.5 m high and 6 m across. They are made of collapsible trellises, secured by leather thongs, over which pieces of felt are stretched and lashed in position. A hole is left directly above the fire pit to allow smoke to escape, but this can be covered at night.

The Bambuti are hunter-gatherers who inhabit the forest regions of central Zaire. Their homes are simple, dome-shaped huts, made from an overlapping layer of leaves laid over a framework of branches.

▲ ▼ ▶ ▼ ▶ ▲ ▼ ▶ ▼ ▶ ▲ ▼ ▶ ▼ ▶ ▲ ▼ ▶ ▼ ▶ ▶

EARTHSHIPS
Recycled Houses
for the Home Planet

by Elizabeth Vitton

Tired of pollution? Then Michael Reynolds
will help you turn a hunk of junk into a home.

Call Michael Reynolds' homes garbage and he
won't be insulted. His homes *are* garbage.

Since the early '70s, Reynolds and his team of
architects have been building houses out of used
tires and old soda pop cans. Called "Earthships,"
the tire homes don't plug into any power lines,
water pipes, or sewage systems. They collect their
own water, have special plumbing, and run on
solar energy.

Earthships can "travel" anywhere—from the
Mojave Desert to the Arctic. But so far, most of the
homes are docked in Taos, New Mexico, where
Reynolds lives.

A Dirty Job

Earthships don't really travel. In fact, they're anchored to one place. Each house is surrounded on three sides by earth. Glass panels cover the exposed south side of the house.

If you want, Reynolds will build your Earthship. Or he'll sell you his do-it-yourself plan. Building one isn't too hard, but it's dirty work: the metre-thick outer walls are made from tires packed full of dirt.

"It's not easy to pound three wheelbarrows full of dirt into each tire," says Pam Freund, who is part of Reynolds' team. And she should know. She's still building her own Earthship.

A packed tire weighs 180 kg! And it takes about 800–900 automobile tires to build one home. It takes even more aluminum cans. The cans are crammed between the tires to fill any gaps. They're also used to make inside walls and room dividers.

"We plaster over the cans and tires with an adobe-like mixture, which is sand, dirt, and a bit of straw," Freund adds. "After it's dry, you can paint the walls any colour you want."

The tire walls and floors (made of brick, flagstone, or concrete) are built to store heat. They absorb sunlight that pours through the glass in winter. When the sun sets, the stored heat comes out of the walls and floor to warm up the house. Heating is a problem only if it's cloudy for more than five days in a row. There's a wood-burning stove or fireplace just in case.

Totally Hot—and Cool

"In February, it can be 30 below outside," says Reynolds, "and we're growing bananas indoors! I even have butterflies flying around through my Earthship."

In summer, he adds, you don't need air conditioning. That's because Earthships are built into the ground. The temperature of the surrounding ground is always 13°C. This keeps the house at 21°C—even on the hottest days.

Sounds like a cool idea, but is it homey? "Yep," answers Kalmy Kendalls. Kalmy, eight, lives with her parents in an Earthship outside Taos. "Even my cat and dog like it here!

"Someone who has never seen an Earthship before might say it looks weird, like a spaceship," Kalmy adds. "But it's just my home. I have my own room. And I can watch movies on our VCR. We have electricity and stuff."

Solar System

Michael Reynolds isn't the first to build a "pit house." (That's a semi-underground home made of dirt.) They've been around for about 10 000 years but his are definitely the first to have VCRs, microwaves, and Jacuzzis.

Earthships run on solar energy. Solar panels on the roof make enough electricity to power all the high-tech gadgets and appliances in the tire home. Even the toilet runs on solar power!

Reynolds' experimental solar toilet "cooks" the waste until it becomes ash. "Have you ever left a pizza in an oven overnight?" he asks. "Well, in the morning all you have left is a bunch of crinkly ash. That's pretty much what the solar toilet does."

The bacteria-free ash can be used to fertilize the plants in the Earthship—and on top of it. (Some people have rooftop gardens.) Reynolds predicts that someday people will grow most of their food, "except bacon and Cheetos."

Where does the water to drink and grow plants come from? "The roof," says Reynolds, pointing upwards. When it rains, the water runs down the sloped roof and into a drain. This sends the water into a tank in the house.

"We then run the rainwater through a series of filters to keep it clean," he explains. "We even have waterfalls in the houses." Used water from the tubs and sinks is recycled into planters that run along the slanted glass walls.

Tired of Pollution

An Earthship is a perfect pollution solution, Reynolds claims. It helps get rid of mountains of tires and cans. Plus, he argues, the earth dwelling doesn't cause more pollution, since it's not hooked up to any gas or oil pipeline, electric plant, or sewage system.

Reynolds says proudly, "You live in a home that grows food, heats and cools itself, makes its own power and water, and deals with its own sewage. This home takes care of you. It's a vessel to sail through the rest of your life in."

But there are still some kinks to work out, he admits. For example, if it's cloudy for a few days in a row, you can't use the solar-powered washing machine. And the solar toilet doesn't "cook" sewage fast enough if you have lots of houseguests.

Reynolds isn't worried. He has big plans for an Earthship that's cheaper, easier to build, more efficient, and homier.

Says Reynolds, "I look at this as an adventure—a voyage." All aboard?

DIRECTION

I was directed by my grandfather
To the East,
    so I might have the power of the bear;
To the South,
    so I might have the courage of the eagle;
To the West,
    so I might have the wisdom of the owl;
To the North,
    so I might have the craftiness of the fox;
To the Earth,
    so I might receive her fruit;
To the Sky,
    so I might lead a life of innocence.

Alonzo Lopez

▲ ▼ ▶ ▼ ▶ ▲ ▼ ▶ ▼ ▶ ▲ ▼ ▶ ▼ ▶ ▲ ▼ ▶ ▼ ▶ ▶

IN THE SHADE
OF A FAMILY TREE

by Robert D. San Souci

Where is home? No matter how many times
they move, people everywhere are interested
in exploring the idea of "home"—their roots
and their ancestors. Robert D. San Souci
looks at this phenomenon from an American
perspective.

People have long been interested in where they
came from—who their ancestors were, where these
people lived, how and why they travelled often
great distances. Recording one's family history is an
ancient tradition. The biblical book Genesis lists the
genealogy (a record of family descent from an ancestor or ancestors) of the great patriarchs (male heads
of families), while the Gospel of St. Matthew lists the
ancestors of Jesus. The *Anglo-Saxon Chronicle*
recounts the descents of the Saxon chieftains.

In traditional Chinese and Japanese ancestor
worship, wooden tablets inscribed with the names
and birth and death dates of the deceased are kept
in the ancestral hall of a clan or in a household
shrine. Many peoples without written records

recall their ancestry through spoken recitations, such as those of African *griots* (elders). It is said that when a griot dies, it is as if a library has been burned to the ground.

Throughout history, keeping accurate accounts of royal family trees has been a vital means of establishing a person's right to rule. From the pharaohs of Egypt to the British monarchs, certain families have steered the course of empires, and the fate of nations has been directly linked to the rulers' bloodlines. Today a person's ancestors may determine his or her place in society.

In Colonial America, settlers from Europe tended to stay in the same place. Children often raised their families near their parents' and grandparents' home. It was easy to keep tabs on where a person came from because there were always relatives and friends to remember.

But as frontiers expanded and new territories opened, transportation became cheaper and less hazardous, people began to move greater distances in greater numbers. Sometimes they moved to better themselves, seeking land, gold, or new business opportunities. Sometimes they were forced to migrate because of war, famine, or social and political unrest. New immigrants arrived from Europe and scattered all across the country. Former slaves from the southern states moved in great numbers after the Civil War.

Today moving is part of life for many families. It is not unusual for an American family to move every few years. In the process, many people lose a sense of their extended family because they lose touch with their ancestors and know little about how their family came to be where it is now.

Yet the desire to know remains a widespread human urge. There is great interest in uncovering one's family tree. Perhaps the most dramatic example was Alex Haley's *Roots*, in which he told how, as a boy in Tennessee, he would listen to his grandmother tell him stories that traced his family back for generations to a man she called "the African."

After 10 years of research, Haley discovered that the name of "the African" was Kunta Kinte; that he had been kidnapped from the village of Juffure in Gambia, West Africa, in 1767; and that he had been carried to Maryland and sold to a Virginia planter. Tracing the family history from his great-great-great-great-great-grandfather to himself, Haley uncovered generations of slaves, freed-men, farmers, blacksmiths, lumber mill workers, Pullman porters, lawyers, architects, and, finally, a writer—himself. Along the way, he discovered numerous relatives, living and dead, eventually even meeting his own African sixth cousins.

For some of us, tracing our family history back to our own roots may uncover a similar thicket of ancestral branches. For others, limited access to relatives or documents may produce a trail that peters out after a generation or two. However far back we can go, the rewards of finding out about our past make the effort worthwhile.

PLANET EARTH

from *The Real World*

Earth—the living planet—and its biosphere appear to be unique in the universe.

If we could hold the earth in the palm of our hand like a fruit, its highest mountains and deepest valleys would feel no rougher to the touch than the skin of a peach. Its atmosphere and immense oceans, some parts of which could drown Mount Everest under a kilometre and a half of water, would scarcely register to the senses even as a film of moisture. Yet it is on this fine tissue of earth, water, and air no more than 15 km thick, from the height of an intercontinental flight to the depths of a diamond mine, that all life depends and owes its origins.

Peeling away that skin of solid ground, water, and air would reveal that the planet seethes in the heat and violence of a nuclear-powered furnace, where even diamonds melt and flow like molasses. New York City rides on a raft of rock that is a mere

35 km above this furnace. In the deep ocean trenches, the crust is thinner still, a bare 5 km. On occasion, the planet is so restless that earthquakes kill hundreds of thousands of people.

But taken as a whole, conditions in the "biosphere" are astonishingly benign, certainly in comparison with our neighbours in the solar system, frigid Mars, or superheated Venus and Mercury.

A series of remarkable coincidences has made this planet a fit place to live on. The earth's distance from the sun, its slight tilt and 24-hour rotation, its very small variation in relief, all mean that the sun's energy is fairly evenly spread in area and duration. The earth's delicate atmosphere is transparent to the sun's most useful light, yet it blocks out most of the meteorites, ultraviolet rays, and cosmic particles whose fearsome energy would destroy life. As a result, a high proportion of the earth's surface is habitable.

It is an extraordinary balancing act. So narrow is the range of conditions in which life can exist that quite small changes, if uncorrected, would have catastrophic results. An increase of a couple of percent in the amount of oxygen in the atmosphere and all plants would burst into flame. A very few degrees' rise in global temperature and much of the world would be drowned. The whole is so interdependent, finely tuned, and self-sustaining that many now believe that the earth is itself alive. They are calling it Gaia, after the Greek goddess who, according to legend, gave birth to the earth.

The planet that humans have inherited has always been a difficult one to cope with. But we have done very much better than simply cope. Earth has also held out a promise, a glorious opportunity for creative human development. We have not just accommodated ourselves to our planet, we have actually transformed it. And in the process we have transformed ourselves.

ACKNOWLEDGEMENTS

Permission to reprint copyright material is gratefully acknowledged. Every reasonable effort to trace the copyright holders of materials appearing in this book has been made. Information that will enable the publisher to rectify any error or omission will be welcomed.

Tashkent from *Some of the Kinder Planets* by Tim Wynne-Jones. Copyright © 1993 by Tim Wynne-Jones. A Groundwood Book/Douglas & McIntyre. Reprinted by permission of Douglas & McIntyre, Toronto and Orchard Books, New York.

How Some Places Got Their Names by Graham Rickard. Extracts from *How Places Got Their Names* by Graham Rickard. Copyright © Young Library Ltd. Reprinted with permission of Young Library Ltd.

Canadian Indian Place Names by Meguido Zola from *Here Is a Poem* published by the League of Canadian Poets. Copyright Meguido Zola. Reprinted by permission of the author.

The Pleasure Periphery from *The Real World*, edited by Bruce Marshall. Copyright © 1991 by Marshall Editions, Ltd. Reprinted by permission of Houghton Mifflin Co. All rights reserved.

Touch the Dragon: A Thai Journal excerpt from *Touch the Dragon: A Thai Journal* by Karen Connelly. Copyright © 1992 Karen Connelly and Turnstone Press. Used with permission.

The Powwow Drum from *Man of Many Colours* by David Campbell. Reprinted by permission of Elliot Chapin, Publisher.

Bang! Bang! It's Tet! by Karen Benoit. Extract from *Somewhere Today* magazine, April 1993, published by the Canadian International Development Agency (CIDA). Used with permission.

Carnival in Trinidad by Vashanti Rahaman from *CRICKET* magazine, February, 1994. Copyright © 1994 Vashanti Rahaman. Reprinted with permission of The Cricket Magazine Group.

Tarma by María Rosa Fort from *Where Angels Glide at Dawn: New Stories from Latin America*, edited by Lori M. Carlson and Cynthia L. Ventura. Copyright © 1990 Lori M. Carlson and Cynthia L. Ventura. Published by J.B. Lippincott, New York. Reprinted by permission of Ellen Levine Literary Agency.

Acknowledgements

Obon: A Family Reunion by Sandy Fox from *FACES* magazine, April 1992 issue: *Ancestors*, © 1992, Cobblestone Publishing, Inc., 7 School St., Peterborough, NH 03458. Reprinted by permission of the publisher.

The Day of the Dead from *Fiesta! Mexico's Great Celebrations* by Elizabeth Silverthorne. Copyright © 1992 by Elizabeth Silverthorne. Used by permission of The Millbrook Press Inc.

Marvellous Monuments by Todd Mercer. Copyright © Nelson Canada, a division of Thomson Canada Limited.

Lights! Camera! Action! The Popular Indian Film by L. Somi Roy from *FACES* magazine, November 1993 issue: *India*, © 1993, Cobblestone Publishing, Inc., 7 School St., Peterborough, NH 03458. Reprinted by permission of the publisher.

Music Around the World by Robert D. San Souci excerpted from *FACES* magazine, December, 1992 issue: *Making Music*, © 1992, Cobblestone Publishing, Inc., 7 School St., Peterborough, NH 03458. Reprinted by permission of the publisher.

Artists of Canada's North from *Northwest Territories* by Lyn Hancock. Published by Grolier Ltd. Copyright © 1993 by Lyn Hancock and Grolier Ltd. Reprinted with permission of the author.

A Selection of Haiku from *Birds, Frogs, and Moonlight*, translated by Sylvia Cassedy and Kunihiro Suetake. Copyright © Sylvia Cassedy.

Grin and Bear It: A Town's Un-fur-gettable Neighbours by John Grossmann from *3–2–1 Contact Magazine*, December 1992. Copyright © 1992 Children's Television Workshop (New York, New York). All rights reserved. Used with permission of CTW.

Trouble in Paradise? from *National Geographic World* magazine. Copyright © January 1993 National Geographic Society. Used with permission.

The Goat Paths from *Collected Poems* by James Stephens published by Macmillan, London and Basingstoke. Reprinted by permission of The Society of Authors on behalf of the copyright owner, Mrs. Iris Wise.

Travelling Pests: Australia's Unwanted Guests from *The Real World*, edited by Bruce Marshall. Copyright © 1991 by Marshall Editions, Ltd. Reprinted by permission of Houghton Mifflin Co. All rights reserved.

Acknowledgements

The Tree Lover by Ruskin Bond from *Young Winter's Tales,* edited by M.R. Hodgkin. Published by Macmillan, London. Copyright © 1970 Ruskin Bond.

The Profile of Africa by Maxine Tynes from *Save the World For Me,* 1991, Pottersfield Press, Porters Lake, Nova Scotia. Copyright © Maxine Tynes. Reprinted with permission of the author.

The Lion's Paw from *The Worlds of a Maasai Warrior* by Tepilit Ole Saitoti. Copyright © 1986 by Tepilit Ole Saitoti. Published by Random House.

Homes on the Move from *The Real World,* edited by Bruce Marshall. Copyright © 1991 by Marshall Editions, Ltd. Reprinted by permission of Houghton Mifflin Co. All rights reserved.

Earthships: Recycled Houses for the Home Planet by Elizabeth Vitton from *3–2–1 Contact Magazine,* November 1993. Copyright 1993 Children's Television Workshop (New York, New York). All rights reserved. Reprinted with permission.

Direction by Alonzo Lopez from *Voices from Wah'kon-Tah* published by International Publishers Inc., 1974. Reprinted by permission of the publishers.

In the Shade of a Family Tree by Robert D. San Souci excerpted from *FACES* magazine, April 1992 issue: *Ancestors,* © 1992, Cobblestone Publishing, Inc., 7 School St., Peterborough, NH 03458. Reprinted by permission of the publisher.

Planet Earth from *The Real World,* edited by Bruce Marshall. Copyright © 1991 by Marshall Editions, Ltd. Reprinted by permission of Houghton Mifflin Co. All rights reserved.

THE EDITORS

Christine McClymont was born in Scotland, but came to Canada at an early age. She has been a junior high teacher, and for many years has compiled anthologies for Nelson Canada series such as Networks, In Context, and Features. Christine enjoys hiking and cross-country skiing, and is actively involved with the Toronto Chamber Society.

James Barry is Chairman of the English Department at Brebeuf College School, a high school in North York, Ontario. He is the editor of the poetry anthologies Themes on the Journey, Departures, Side by Side, and Poetry Express, as well as an annual student writing anthology, Triple Bronze. Besides teaching, his special interests are sports (especially hockey), music, and student writing.

Berenice Wood is an instructor in the Faculty of Education at the University of Victoria. She has been an English Department Head and Secondary English Coordinator, and was responsible for developing the current Language Arts–English provincial curriculum for the B.C. Ministry of Education. Her interests include gardening, writing, and all generations of Star Trek.